My
TOM
a memoir

By Ruth Morgan

*To Jan —
Enjoy the book,
enjoy life!
Love,
Ruth Morgan*

Publisher
R.W. Morgan Press
Port Richey, Florida

Ruth Morgan
My Tom - A Memoir

Cover by Marcia Revak

ISBN 0-0770507-0-0

Printed June 2006

DEDICATION

To all who met Tom and became a part of him

ACKNOWLEDGMENTS

My thanks go to my family and friends who supported this effort. I am especially grateful to my brother Tom Wing for his editorial advice and to my nephew-in-law Bill Austin for his suggestions. Two librarians Ann Coppola and Linda Rothstein of the Pasco County Library System in Florida gave generously of their time and expertise to answer all my questions. I am indebted to Ursula Bracker who assuaged my anxieties about the publication process and to Henry Fletcher who clarified some of the complexities in concert band arrangements. My gratitude must also be expressed to Victor Ramirez and his wife Rosalia of Tri-Arts Studio, Inc. Their extreme patience extended to me during my many revisions was Job-like. With their warmth and affability they provided a comfort level that was greatly appreciated. All the individuals mentioned above helped produce this book.

FOREWORD

To find a phrase defining a man is not easy, but for Tom Morgan one does come to mind - joie de vivre. Not wanting a life of quiet desperation he sought one with satisfying efforts. This was manifested in an eagerness to be an active human being rather than a passive one. Never wanting to regret not trying, he pursued anything that piqued his interest. He wanted to explore any activity, usual or unusual. He did not have to be the best; he wanted to do his best to test his limits. With this motivation he traveled diverse paths that became a journey leading to this singular life, one that was filled with enjoyment and satisfaction.

The words unconventional, irreverent, undaunted, irrepressible, unselfish, witty, scrupulous, sympathetic characterized his way of life. When he transformed his joy of living into the joy of sharing, he endeared himself to all involved in that experience. His enthusiasm put a smile on the faces of all around him. Tom's sense of humor appeared, expectedly and often unexpectedly, in many things he did.

Knowing the memorable life Tom had, I felt compelled to write about him. This book is part of his legacy and my memorial to Tom Morgan.

Contents

Prologue - Kismet   1

Part One - Madame Butterfly   3

Part Two - A Teacher's Teacher   9

Part Three - Chess Mentor   27

Part Four - Eager Athlete   33

Part Five - Eveready Fisherman   47

Part Six - Creative Humorist   67

Part Seven - IRS Auditee   77

Part Eight - Belated Genealogist   81

Part Nine - Accomplished Amateur   89

Part Ten - Responsible Godfather   97

Epilogue - Prophetic Dream   103

Prologue

Kismet

Marriage was always a goal for women in my circle. Two girls from my high school class were married the year after graduation. Most of us never woke up every morning making a conscious effort to seek a lifetime mate that day. But this thought was always lurking in our minds. However, my objective was not the institution of marriage but a man for a life partner who would help to create a happy partnership. Matrimony was not the end; it was the means to an end. In fact, wedded bliss was my third objective. The first was to get an education. The second was to get established in a profession. After all, we graduated from college at a time when a woman could make a comfortable living, be a breadwinner herself, and survive independently without a man. We were not our mothers.

The last place I thought to find a husband was in the work area, my work place, a public high school, Lincoln High School in Jersey City, New Jersey. It was not impossible but rather improbable. Then, Tom Morgan entered the scene as an addition to the faculty of Lincoln. He was just a new teacher in my department. New members of the staff received some special attention from me initially to help them adjust to the new environment, new routines, new colleagues. Answering all my memos, Tom wrote replies that were neat, thoughtful, and humorous. Those last two elements made me sit up and raise my eyebrows. Hmmh! Interesting!

We were both members of the Jersey City Federation of Teachers, a local of the American Federation of Teachers affiliated with the American Federation of Labor/Congress of Industrial Organizations, the AFL/CIO. Attending union meetings, we gravitated toward each other to chat. One thing led naturally to another and to the rest of the story, this life with Tom Morgan.

In the next few years four other Lincoln High School teachers found their spouses among the other faculty members in this building. One could say that this school was a mating institution as well as an educational one.

Part One

Madame Butterfly

When the man asks the woman the question, "Will you marry me?" and before the woman can reply, he elaborates, " I can't promise you money, but I do promise you lots of love and lots of laughs." How could I, the woman, resist? I capitulated to those promises readily and eagerly said, "Yes!"

Of course, my acceptance was not a rash response. The man, Tom Morgan, and I, Ruth Wing, had been dating over a year and found much common ground - morals, ethics, standards, practices, values, looks, personality, grooming, fitness, quick wit (on Tom's part), quick appreciation of wit (on my part), sense of humor (on Tom's part), good humor (on my part).

And, yes, underlying everything was that magical spark that ignited the flame of desire to live together as man and wife. Thus began our journey to discover happiness through love, fun, and adventure for thirty one years.

Our courtship was traditional, although we were not the usual characters in this kind of plot. Tom was Irish American; I was Chinese American. He was Catholic; I was Protestant. Tom was assigned as an English teacher in Lincoln High School in Jersey City, New Jersey, after earning his bachelor's degree while on a full time job with the U.S. Treasury Department. I was head of the English Department in Lincoln High School. Some teachers perceived this position as an administrative post, but that perception was far from accurate. So, there were Tom and I thrown together by the fates in the same school and in the same department. After working with him for a year, I told my closest colleague in the school that Tom was a man I could be interested in because he had many admirable traits. The interest proved to be mutual and we started dating. We did not want to be known as an "item" in school to avoid being subjected to the scrutiny of all when a romance appears on the scene. We were circumspect in school as our relationship deepened. Or so we thought! One day Tom led a discussion in his freshman class at the conclusion of studying "Romeo and Juliet." When asked what they liked best about the play, the answers were predictable: the boys enjoyed the action-fights, duels; the girls preferred the love interest - the balcony scene, the star-crossed lovers. Now Tom could not resist and teased, "Oh, you girls, all you can think of is romance." That last word was pronounced with a bit of disdain as if to say there were other elements to find in literature.

A girl in a small voice close to him murmured, "Well, I don't know about that, Mr. Morgan." He quickly turned to her, ready to explore her literary thoughts and asked, "What do you mean?" She lowered her eyelids, fluttered her eyelashes, looked at him sideways, tilted her lips in a knowing smile, and softly said, "You know, Madame Butterfly?" A bit rattled by that personal reference, Tom hastily retreated, "Well, we'll move on to the new work." End of that literary discussion.

The significance of that allusion was not lost on us. This young student lived in a deprived, disadvantaged neighborhood with all the evils that thrive in such an area, but some how she became familiar with the story of Madame Butterfly. Learning from this experience, probably a rare one for an underprivileged youngster, she applied her knowledge intelligently and humorously. She teased the teacher. Tom was hoisted on his own petard. There should always be the hope for our youth to be educated regardless of their circumstances.

Before Tom and I could announce our marital intentions to the world, we had to tell our parents. Tom's family expected this development because he had brought me home for dinner. This social meeting indicated a special relationship. His parents treated me cordially and made me feel quite comfortable. We exchanged pleasantries easily. As a good guest, I complimented Tom's mother on her cooking. Pleased, she offered me more helpings of food. As a good guest, I accepted. After Tom had driven me home, he asked his father, "Well, Dad, what do you think of Ruth?"

Without hesitation he replied, "God bless her, she can eat!" Tom took that as the Good Housekeeping Seal of Approval.

On the other hand, my parents had a reaction that was diametrically opposite to that of Tom's parents. My family was a matriarchal unit; my mother was the spokesperson for the parental pair. Mama had a control over her six children that was a mastery of subterfuge. The worst thing we could hear her say in a quiet statement that ended any discussion or dispute was, "Don't make your father angry." And, of course, we never did. We acquiesced unhesitatingly to the implied threat and just never crossed that line. To this day we never challenged him. He probably would not know how to handle it. Mama made sure that would not happen. She subdued us with the concept, "The threat is worse than the execution." Cleverly, wisely, covertly, she led her children, six of us, to believe that our father was the final arbiter on all issues. To Papa's credit he never did anything to discredit that belief. He was happy not to deal with the children. Mama would say, "We'll see what your father thinks about it." We neither saw nor heard any discussion between them. Later, Mama would announce, "This is what your father wants." Today I really doubt Papa had any serious input in these "talks." Sure, Mama explained the details, but undoubtedly she voiced her opinion and Papa would agree. And that was that.

On the night Tom came to my home to ask for my hand in marriage, he brought a couple of pounds of seedless green grapes. Mama washed them and put them on the round formica topped table in the kitchen. With the four of us sitting there, Papa started to eat the grapes and murmured something about their sweetness, savoring them. After a few pleasantries Tom broached the subject of his love for me and his wish to marry me. Mama was no dummy and was not too surprised to hear these avowals. She calmly stated her opposition to the union because Tom was not Chinese. She listed the obvious differences in culture, mores, practices, beliefs, religion. All would be too many obstacles to a happy marriage. What seemed like an eternity, but was probably more like an hour and a half, followed with pro's offered by Tom and me, con's posited by Mama.

5

Papa kept popping grapes into his mouth, characteristically relieved to have the decisions made by Mama. Tom was eternally grateful to him for staying neutral for whatever reasons and leaving Mama as the lone voice of opposition. Mama finally capitulated, "I see you two are not going to change your minds. So be it." Ex cathedra. Tom really argued with determination and persistence to win my parents' approval, no matter how reluctant, for our marriage.

Three of my siblings had Chinese spouses. My partner would be the first non-Chinese member in our family. They had a difficult time accepting this union, but eventually they did and followed my mother's lead in yielding to the inevitable.

A couple of months later my mother and father hosted a party for the Morgan and Wing families. During that evening when our parents had their first face-to-face meeting, they had long conversations. Their major topics were family and children, particularly Tom for his parents and me for my parents. At the end of the evening Mama told me that from these talks with Mr. and Mrs. Morgan she thought that Tom was a good person. That was the highest praise she could give to any one. And he proved her right. In the years that followed she often said in her broken English, "I lob (love) you, Tom."

That Christmas of 1968 Tom gave me a beautiful diamond solitaire surrounded by six prongs, popularly known as the Tiffany setting. My first choice was a ruby, my second an emerald. But with engagement rings this iconoclast was orthodox. Tom wanted me to have a diamond. And so it was a diamond I wore. We were officially engaged, ready for the world.

On the first day of school after Tom had given me the ring, I signed the attendance book which really required two hands. Colleagues who were waiting to do the same noticed the ring immediately. The hubbub started.

They, "Who's the lucky guy?"

I, "Tom."

They, "Tom who?"

I, "Tom Morgan."

They, in amazement, "Our Tom Morgan!?"

I, with a smile, "Yes, our Tom Morgan, now my Tom Morgan."

Jaws dropped, mouths gaped, tongues wagged.

The reactions to the news of our engagement were varied at the school. After my ring was seen at the sign-in book, the word spread and preceded our presence everywhere we went in the building. I fared much better than Tom. My peers were delighted and peppered me with wishes for happiness, comments of surprise, questions about plans. However, Tom did not do so well because he had an evangelical bent. His enthusiasm for anything transformed into an advocacy - for fishing, chess, bachelorhood. He was dubbed the Billy Graham of the bachelors among the male staff. He often reminded the single men of the blessed state of the Benedicks. He did protest too much. Now, this leader of the unmarried men had committed himself to the state of matrimony! Tom braced himself. He knew what was coming. He ran the gauntlet and suffered the gamut of taunts and jeers about the fallen idol, the vociferous spokesman for bachelors soon to become a bridegroom, an advocate who didn't practice what he preached, a traitor to his followers! This bombardment lasted for several days, but Tom took it with grace. He had to; he had no choice.

Students reacted predictably. Girls smiled approvingly, knowingly. Boys chose to ignore the news. Two of the nicest students I ever taught, Pamela Bryant and Perveen Rizvi, also had English with Tom. They gave us a present of six wine glasses etched in an abstract pattern reminiscent of Indian decoration. Perveen's family emigrated from Pakistan. This set of glasses was the only gift students gave us, and it was among the most beautiful of all we received. These two youngsters were among the loveliest teenagers I ever had. They had all the desirable traits: attitude, character, ethics, habits, manners, and the icing on the cake - brains and beauty! A formidable combination. All parents would be lucky to have them as daughters or daughters-in-law. I consider myself most fortunate to have been their teacher.

So Tom and I became man and wife on March 29, 1969. That was a memorable year. We tied the knot, Neil Armstrong walked on the moon, taking one step for man, one leap for mankind, the New York Jets won the Super Bowl, the New York Knicks won the NBA Championship, the New York Mets won the World Series. And we merrily started our life together. What a year, what a beginning!

Tom and Ruth Morgan, March 29, 1969

Part Two
A Teacher's Teacher

Tom was born in the Bronx, New York. He fondly called it "da Bronx," a pejorative term accepted only by and from a native Bronxite. His mother, Margaret Reilly, was born in Manhattan of Irish parents. Unfortunately, she was orphaned before she was ten. Her mother, Nora Mullins O'Reilly, died after World War 1; her father, Jeremiah O'Reilly (later Reilly), died a few years later. Now alone in the world, young Margaret Reilly was left with Mrs. McCarthy, a widow who owned the rooming house where the Reillys lived and took care of the orphan. Tom's father, Thomas Morgan, was born in County Roscommon, Ireland, and escaped the British conscription of Irish soldiers by emigrating to England, then to the United States. He landed in Manhattan and found lodging in the boarding house where Margaret Reilly worked and lived. In a few years they married and had two children: Peggy and Tom. Tom's dad called his wife "Mam" and a "narrowback" meaning first generation American born of Irish parents.

Tom received his education in Catholic schools attending Sts. Peter and Paul Elementary School in the Bronx, Cardinal Hayes High School in Manhattan, and Seton Hall University in East Orange, New Jersey.

As a senior in Cardinal Hayes he was recruited by the U.S. Treasury Department. After some years in the department he thought chasing drug dealers, setting up "drops" that did not materialize often, and breaking down doors to apartments of drug users did not offer too much job satisfaction. Once on a raid that led to a chase of the culprits, Tom, being the youngest, raced ahead of his colleagues. Running at top speed to catch the perpetrators, he heard bullets whiz by his ears! Suddenly the realization hit him-these bullets came from behind him! These bullets were fired by his fellow agents! "Killed by friendly fire!" flashed through his mind. He quickly slowed down to let the gunners catch up to him and go on to make the arrest. He also became aware of corruption and politicking practiced by some agents. Tom wanted no association with these immoral, self-aggrandizing elements. Not seeing himself put twenty five years into this kind of work, he decided on a career move. What was another vocation for him? He believed that teaching was a profession of integrity, honesty, and honor. These personal traits he could bring to the job and have a satisfying career. When he reached that decision, he enrolled at Seton Hall University in the evening division for a teaching degree. Continuing to work for the department through his junior year, he saved enough money to attend college full time for his last year and speed up the acquisition of his bachelor's degree. He existed on peanut butter and jelly sandwiches and persevered. Eight years after graduation from high school he very proudly accepted his Bachelor of Science degree.

Tom was now among the ranks of the unemployed. As a resident of Jersey City he applied in that district for positions to teach high school English. He found a job immediately at S nyder High School. The next year he filled a vacancy in Lincoln High School.

A good-looking, clean-cut man, Tom had green eyes, even features,

Tom in his fedora with Nicholas, his godson, and Ruth

Tom in a jockey cap

fair skin sprinkled with freckles. He had an athletic build with broad shoulders that tapered to his waist, slim hips, and well shaped legs. On top of his head was a Charlie Brown curlicue of medium brown hair; in his late twenties he was balding. That was the reason he wore hats all the time. He had all kinds of headgear - baseball caps, watch caps, jockey caps, but he loved the fedora. Wearing that hat he looked like Tom Landry, former coach of the Dallas Cowboys, a comparison he enjoyed. He liked Landry for his looks, his grooming, his clothes, his attitude, his philosophy, but above all for his fedora.

As an English teacher Tom worked diligently, planning activity based on the courses of study, preparing daily lessons plans, checking homework daily, grading all written assignments that required corrections and revisions. An instructor at Seton Hall gave invaluable advice that served Tom well during his teaching career. "Remember, one third of your students will learn because of you, one third will learn in spite of you, the last third, well, just entertain them." That statement summarized the realistic results of teaching. Some students will be aided, guided, and hopefully inspired by the teacher. Some students will be already academically able, mentally sharp, and do well without too much help from the teacher. And some, one third, how depressing, will be unreachable by the teacher no matter what he or she does. Accept that fact. Don't take it personally. Amuse that last group somehow or other which could prevent them from being too disruptive and maybe help them enjoy your class no matter what the reason. Because of that last third, Tom successfully injected some humorous comments in all his classes. The students found him amusing and even eccentric, a word which a few of his students used to describe him, appropriately and frequently.

Even with that humor or because of it Tom was an effective teacher. One year PBS ran a series on the rating of high schools in the Newark, New Jersey, area and invited a group of bright juniors from Lincoln High School to discuss the quality of their education on television. They answered questions about programs, buildings, extra-curricular activities, and faculty. When asked about their teachers, they responded that some were average, some were not so good, and a few were very good. In fact, a few students said they were privileged to have been taught by one they considered the best in the school. Of course, the moderator tactfully did not ask for the identity of that teacher in a public forum. Many of us were watching that program and the next day the principal asked those students for the name of that best teacher in their opinion. Yes, it was Tom!

Tom believed in Francis Bacon's statement:

> "Reading maketh a full man, conference a readye
> man, writing an exacte man."

With this as a personal motto, he practiced what he preached. Tom was a prolific writer - abstracting books he valued chapter by chapter, annotating all books he read. As a teacher he required all his students to have a notebook filled with notes on the literature and the grammar studied in class, returned homework, all original essays and book reports with corrected revisions. In essence, the notebook was a compilation of all their work for that year, serious stuff. To reinforce that fact, the notebook became an important part of the marking period grade. This was a necessary incentive for the students to keep a notebook. If there is no follow up by the teacher, that usually leads to no work by the student. Therefore, at the end of each of the four marking periods Tom collected the notebooks from all the pupils in his five classes, brought them home, read them, annotated them, and graded them, which obviously entailed a great deal of time at home. He required these notebooks every year he taught. How effective was this method? Tom had no idea, no concrete data to measure the effectiveness of this teaching technique. However, he firmly believed that writing makes the exact man. It worked for him, optimistically, he hoped it would work for his students, perhaps for two thirds of them.

Once he brought these notebooks on a winter vacation in Venezuela to complete them for the marking period that ended the week of our return. One of his suitcases was filled with these books. He had them all read and graded by the time we arrived at the airport for our flight back to the United States. Unhappily, we learned that our plane would be late. Waiting in the lounge with our luggage, we saw a local rifle-toting officer with a drug-sniffing dog ready to do his duty. Bored by our long delay, most of us watched this dog. There was a young, attractive black couple with new, expensive luggage. After Fido examined their new bags, he sniffed at the couple, then raised his head and returned to their first bag. Tom and I nudged each other, our interest heightened by the dog's need to recheck this suitcase. Then, in time-honored tradition he made the classic move of lifting one hind leg and spraying these gorgeous new bags. The dog certainly did his duty - he heeded the call of nature. The couple was furious and demanded recourse. The rest of us were happy the dog did not single out our luggage to relieve himself. Naturally, Tom imagined the reactions of his pupils upon hearing the teacher's explanation, "I can't return your notebooks because a Venezuelan dog urinated on them!"

In a twenty six year teaching career, an educator has many experiences, some memorable, some forgettable. Tom had a few unforgettable ones.

Tom had a journalism class and with it the obligatory extra-curricular activity of being advisor to the school newspaper, The Lincoln Leader. He used this class as a workshop for his students to practice journalism.

In 1978 soccer was quickly developing a fan base in New Jersey. The world's most popular sport made a mark in this nation with a league that included a metropolitan area team, the Cosmos. Soccer soon became an athletic activity in some of the private and public schools in New Jersey, but not in the schools in Jersey City. Fortunately, a convergence of events occurred - a school newspaper, an advisor who was alert to opportunities for his students to have hands-on experiences, and positive public attitudes toward an issue. The issue - include soccer in the athletic program for all public high schools in Jersey City. Tom's plan was to have The Lincoln Leader spearhead a campaign for such inclusion. The journalism students, most of them on the newspaper staff, committed themselves to this cause. The newspaper's student editor, Mark Williams, was hard-working, self-motivated, and persistent. Guided by Tom, Mark sent letters to the Superintendent of Schools and the district's Athletic Director in which he outlined the need and value of having soccer as a sport in the city's high schools. To support this position, Mark, members of the newspaper staff, and the other journalism students collected over 800 signatures, more than half the student body in Lincoln, petitioning the Board of Education for a soccer program in the high schools. After enlisting the aid of the school's Student Council, he took the next step and invited the newspaper staffs and Student Councils of the four other Jersey City public high schools to join Lincoln High School in this effort. The young editor even went through the procedure of being placed on the agenda for a public meeting of the Jersey City Board of Education to present his case. Two years later the Board of Education instituted soccer as a part of the athletic programs in the five public high schools in Jersey City.

The Lincoln Leader, a high school newspaper, advocated a change. Then its staff thoughtfully developed a plan, carefully executed the plan, persistently followed the plan, and it all paid off. The idea of a high school newspaper became a reality. One student publication effected an improvement in the athletic program for an entire school district. What an achievement! Journalism at work; journalism at its best!

Mark received a scholarship for a summer program in journalism at a New Jersey college. With that on his resume he got a job the next summer with the Jersey Journal, the newspaper with the largest circulation in Jersey City, the second largest city in New Jersey, the most densely populated state in the union. Mark went on to college in Boston, majored in communications, and even worked as a broadcaster on the radio station for the college.

Occasionally, the unexpected opportunity appears. Would you ever imagine the Manhattan Yacht Club sponsoring students from a Jersey City school servicing a disadvantaged area to crew as members in the 1989 Tall Ships Race from London, (yes, England), to Hamburg, (yes, Germany)?   This was stuff out of fiction! Well, it happened. That unique chance came when Michael W. Fortenbaugh, the Commodore of the Manhattan Yacht Club, learned about Lincoln High School from a reporter with WOR-TV and offered this sailing trip to three Lincoln High youngsters.

The principal of Lincoln asked Tom to take on the responsibility for the selection of these would-be sailors. He composed this flyer to give the details about the event and pique the interest of the students.

Tall Ships Race 1989

Through the sponsorship of the Manhattan Yacht Club and with the help of WWOR, Channel 9, A+ Challenge, three students from Lincoln High School will be selected to join the crew of a tall ship competing this summer in the Tall Ships Race from London, England, to Hamburg, Germany, to celebrate the 800th Anniversary of London's incorporation as a municipality.

Three students and six alternates, all of whom must be at least 16 years of age, will be candidates to join the professional crew of the motor yacht, "Creighton's Naturally," an 80 foot ship made for speed and comfort. The alternates will supply the substitutes for any of the three finalists who cannot participate because of an illness or a personal emergency. All nine selectees will sail with the Manhattan Yacht Club to test their sea legs and comfort with sailing conditions. While these students need not be seasoned sailors, they are expected to assist actively with the day-to-day operations of the vessel. As on all ships, the skipper has the first, last, and final word on all matters. His word and authority are absolutely unquestioned on board.

Festivities will attend both ends of the trip with a few days in the middle for the race itself. The Manhattan Yacht Club will pay for all expenses including the round trip to Europe. However, the club will not defray the cost of passports for this journey. The Lincoln High School staff will assist in the acquisition and payment for the passports. Lincoln students will be the first Americans ever to compete in this race and would have the opportunity not only to represent their country in this prestigious event but also to meet their peers from high schools around the world.

Do you have a sense of adventure? Would you like to be chosen for this fantastic trip? Do you think you're the right one to represent your country in this event? If the answer is "Yes," then here's what to do. Write an essay of 150 to 200 words telling what qualities you have that would recommend you for the selection and what impressions of Americans you would like to leave with your fellow students joining you in this international endeavor. The deadline for entries is May 25, 1989. Submit your entry to your English teacher who will forward it to Mr. Morgan. Parental permission is required. Your parent must sign the back of your essay to indicate that permission is granted for your participation in this competition.

Thirteen students responded and each had to be evaluated so three could be chosen. To assist him, Tom enlisted a group of faculty members and sent them this letter to guide them through the selection process.

Tall Ships Race 1989
Essay Evaluation

Congratulations! Your reputation has endorsed you as one of the sterling evaluators of the Tall Ships Essay Competition. Since English teachers have been sought by candidates in this contest to help them develop their essays, we believe that it is necessary to remove English teachers from the Essay Evaluation Committee to thwart any charge of favoritism. Thus, we are relying on you as a professional to rate the following essays on a scale of one to five with five being the highest and one being the lowest. Keep in mind that the three students selected from this competition must not only represent Lincoln High School in Jersey City but also the United States of America. It is safe to assume that much media attention is going to be centered on this event. We want to be sure that the three finalists not only reflect positively upon their school but also on their country.

Each essay has a circle in the upper right hand corner. You have only to place a number in that circle to reflect your opinion with five as the highest and one as the lowest. Please rate each essay on merit according to how well the essay question posed was answered. Try not to let your familiarity with the student influence your decision. The essay should be rated holistically which means that little importance is given to spelling and mechanical rules for proper expression and greater importance is given to content.

The essay score represents one half of the grade to determine the selection of the finalist. The remaining half will be decided by the interview.

We have been given very little time to put this competition together; consequently, it is important that you rate the essays this weekend and place your number ratings in the circles provided. These ratings must be returned to Mr. Morgan the morning of Tuesday, May 30, 1989, to prepare for the interviews that must be completed by the next day, Wednesday, May 31, 1989.

This contest represents a phenomenal opportunity for three Lincoln High School students. It may never come again. We want to do our best.

Thanks for helping. We're often asked to go the extra mile for our students. This is just another one of those demands that others take for granted but which we so readily give because we care.

T. Morgan
Eng. Dept.

Tall Ships Race finalists Tonya Falls, left, Ethan James, center, and Myron Cooper with Tom in the rear

The three finalists were Myron Cooper, Tonya Falls, and Ethan James. They trained, crewed their ship, and did not suffer seasickness. That last in itself was a personal victory for these landlubbers. Lincoln High School was proud of their representatives in this international sailing event.

Who among their peers could say as teen-agers that they flew to London, partied in London and Hamburg, and sailed on a tall ship with English teen-agers and professional sailors? It is unlikely that they will ever encounter such an adventure again on such a global scale. This was a first for Lincoln High School and a first for New Jersey.

Just as this was a unique chance for the students, so was it for the teachers. They seized this opportunity and worked eagerly to get three young people on board this ship. Under severe time constraints, these veteran teachers completed the required tasks and chose the three sailors to give them a once-in-a-lifetime experience.

High school teachers can enjoy gratifying fulfillment. For a short time they educate, tutor, mentor, nurture teen-agers, then send them, hopefully, on to a successful journey through life. These teachers involved with the 1989 Tall Ships Race quietly reveled in their noble effort that had wonderful results. They did not work for public praise which they did not receive anyway. They knew theirs was a job well done. That was their personal satisfaction and all they needed. So many teachers are our unsung heroes.

Then, there was Daniel Robinson, a pupil in one of Tom's sophomore English classes. His attitude, work ethics, body language, and spotty attendance did not portend a potential star student. After an absence of several days Daniel appeared; Tom stated how glad he was to see the young man and hoped he would attend more regularly which could lead to a passing grade. In a couple of days, Daniel could not help himself and made a disrespectful remark that prompted a reprimand from Tom who did not want the group's discipline dismantled. Daniel turned surly and used the favorite Anglo-Saxon four letter expletive, essentially challenging the teacher's authority. This class had been responding well to Tom who had carefully molded a respectful attitude to him. Yet, they were quietly eager to see how he would meet Daniel's challenge. A fight's a fight! How is it going to end? That is the eternal struggle between pupil and teacher every single day. Every teacher knows this and knows it can happen any day in any class. If the teacher wins, so does the class. If the teacher loses, it is a lost year for most of the students, particularly those who don't have the self-discipline to resist external influences. The teacher should be prepared. And Tom was. He calmly picked up his roll book, the teacher's life-line, and placidly asked Daniel to step out of the room with him. Daniel enjoyed this attention, knowing the eyes of all his peers were on him and almost strutted from the room ahead of Tom. Closing the door slowly behind him, Tom casually looked up and down the corridor, saw no one in sight, and walked Daniel away from the door so the students in the class could neither see nor hear them. He leaned toward Daniel, nose to nose, not touching him, and quietly hissed through his teeth, "Daniel, if you don't get your _____in' ass into that _____in' class and _____in' behave, I'm going to take your _____in' ass down to the _____in' gym and kick it off every _____in' wall! Do you _____in' understand me?!?" With every _____in' usage by Tom, Daniel's eyes got wider and wider. Teachers were not supposed to say that word! It's reserved exclusively for pupils to use and upset authority figures. Daniel squeezed his back against the wall, gulped, and amazingly said, "Yes, Mr. Morgan." They returned to the classroom and Tom resumed teaching. Daniel was fine in class for a few days. Unfortunately, he disappeared again.

Some time later, the school principal called Tom into his office. When Tom walked in, he saw the principal, the boys' disciplinarian, Daniel, and a man he immediately presumed to be Daniel's father. Tom sized up the situation and seized the initiative. Before anyone could speak, he strode to the unknown man, extended his hand, and said,

"You must be Daniel's father. I'm so happy to meet you and have this chance to talk to you. I've been meaning to call you and discuss Daniel's poor attendance. Daniel has potential and with better attendance and the two of us helping him, he still has time to turn things around."

The father was nonplussed. The principal took over, summoned the dignity of his office, and intoned,

"Well, Mr. Morgan, Daniel has brought serious charges against you."

"Charges? Against me!?!" The "me" was expressed in a syllable and a half with much surprise by Tom.

"Daniel said you cursed at him using the 'f' word," the principal stated.

Tom looked directly at the principal and asked, "During my more than ten years teaching here at Lincoln have you ever heard that charge against me?"

"No," answered the principal.

"Do you think I would ever curse at a student?" questioned Tom.

"Well, of course not," replied the principal.

Tom turned to the disciplinarian and asked, "Has any student ever brought this charge against me in all the years we've worked together here?"

"No," was the reply.

"Do you even think that word is in my vocabulary?" Tom continued with the disciplinarian.

"Well, no," he said.

Now Tom narrowed his eyelids, stared directly into Daniel's eyes, and indignantly asked, "How could you say anything like that about me, Daniel!?!"

Daniel had no chance to respond. By this time his father, listening to the testimony of two school officials, had heard enough. He stood up, walked over to Daniel, and scolded him, "How could you bring me in here to listen to your false charge against Mr. Morgan? I had to take time off from work for this. Wait till I get you at home. Go back to your class now."

Befuddled, stunned, Daniel's eyes welled up with tears and he left.

Mr. Robinson stood up, shook hands with everybody, and

apologized for taking their time to listen to what apparently was an unfounded charge. To Tom, he said, "I'm glad to meet you, Mr. Morgan, and maybe we can do something with Daniel."

"I certainly hope so," Tom replied.

All said their goodbyes.

When Tom left the office and walked down the corridor, he saw Daniel drooped over a small statue of Lincoln sitting on a log, reading a book. Tom, devilish, daring Tom, checked that no one was in the hallway and seized this chance to apply the "coup de grace." He walked up to Daniel and in an avuncular fashion put his arm gently around the young man's shoulder and whispered into his ear, "Now you know who to _____ with, Daniel." Daniel's shoulders collapsed into his chest, a movement of utter defeat. Tom strolled away with a serene demeanor, but with the blare of 76 trombones in his ears. Later at home he threw his roll book, the teacher's life-line, into the air and yelled, "This day has made my year!" And it was only October.

By the way, Daniel did not come to class anymore and, predictably, that class worked well the rest of the year. Tom was right, that day made a good year for him and for the students in that class.

At the end of one marking period, a pupil was dissatisfied with the grade he received in Tom's class. He showed his dissatisfaction by scratching his opinion in big letters on the hood of Tom's car, "You ain't shit, Mr. Morgan." Even dismayed with the damage, Tom left that disparaging message there because it showed a certain amount of respect. The pupil addressed him as Mr. Morgan. Also, the pupil used correct spelling and punctuation. Tom thought of it as his motto. Practically, he saw that comment left no room for more graffiti in case another pupil wanted to follow suit.

Another student, Brenda, was already a legend when she entered Tom's sophomore class. She was neither nasty nor offensive, just loud and disruptive. But she had a saving grace, she wanted to learn. Brenda proved to be a good student. Encouraged by her early academic progress, she decided it was time to challenge Tom and establish her dominance in this class.

At the beginning of one session, Brenda blurted from her seat in the back of the room, no need for her to raise her hand to speak,

"Mr. Morgan, I have to go to the bathroom."

"I'm busy with attendance, Brenda." Tom did not have to look up to know who had spoken. "Ask again in a little while."

The rest of the students perked up, at attention. They knew this was Brenda's opening salvo, their interest was piqued. Who was going to win this contest - student or teacher?

Tom, the experienced teacher, recognized the challenge, but he could not be completely sure this request to use the bathroom was not legitimate, particularly for girls. His tactic was to delay, not to issue an outright rejection. If it was truly a necessity, the student would wait a minute or two, then repeat the request. Many times Tom wrote a bathroom pass after determining it was necessary. The teacher wanted to be sure the student's purpose was based on a legitimate physiological urge, not an illegitimate social urge. And, if the pupil did not make another attempt to leave the class, so much the better.

But this was Brenda. She started grumbling in her seat.

"Mr. Morgan, I have to go," she shouted,

"But, Brenda, I'm not finished," Tom answered quietly.

Hearing that, she marched up to Tom near his desk and said emphatically, "I have to go now!"

The other pupils were almost sitting on the edges of their seats. This was show time, Brenda's show, and they eagerly awaited this show-down. O.K. Corral in Lincoln! This was fun!

A teacher who shared this room with Tom kept a box of tissues and some paper cups in a desk drawer. Noting the emphatic "now," Tom quickly bent over to this desk drawer, took out the box of tissues, a cup, and placed them on the desk. Without looking at Brenda, he continued with his task. The rest of the class erupted with laughter.

Tom won the battle, but did he win the war?

Brenda, momentarily speechless, harrumphed her way back to her seat.

"I'm going to tell my mother on you, Mr. Morgan. We'll take you to court and charge you with Sagittarius rape."

Brenda received an A on her last vocabulary test. Obviously, usage was not her strength.

Keeping a straight face, Tom's response was, "I'll be sure to get in touch with my astrologer before we go to court." The humor in this reply was lost on everybody.

This was probably Brenda's first loss in her favorite academic sport, teacher confrontations. The difference here was her loss in the eyes of her peers. While she was out to victimize Tom, the teacher, his wordless, spontaneous put down in "bathroom" humor and the reaction of her fellow classmates disarmed her. Without saying a word Tom enjoyed not only his victory, no small feat to set the tone in the relationship between student and teacher, but also the respect Brenda showed by addressing him as Mr. Morgan and seeking his permission to leave the room. Tom guessed right this time, Brenda stayed in the room the entire period. And this incident was not repeated. So, Tom did win the war, too.

That advice from his college instructor about the use of humor in the classroom proved invaluable. The bonus in this case was not only winning over Brenda or one third of the class, but also the entire group.

Tom did have a star pupil, Anna, who was in that group that did not need too much help from her teacher. Anna and her mother emigrated from Poland and settled in Jersey City. After a few years in elementary school, Anna entered Lincoln as a freshman. With intelligence supported by aptitude and attitude she learned to read, write, and speak English better than most of her classmates who were born in this country. An ideal student in every way, it was almost a given that she would excel academically. Anna lived the immigrant's dream in America by working toward her goals. Her hard work, determination, and persistence paid off. She was valedictorian of her class and the recipient of a fully funded four year scholarship to the prestigious Massachusetts Institute of Technology. Is that a success story?!! Before starting MIT, she wrote Tom a letter acknowledging him as one English teacher she would always remember. Tom considered himself lucky that Anna was one his students.

Mark, the three sailors, Daniel, Brenda, and Anna, all in their own way, provided memorable experiences that punctuated Tom's career. These students gave him that personal, at times, exquisite satisfaction that made teaching a worthwhile profession. How fortunate he made the right career choice.

In 1991 Tom was elected as Lincoln High School's Hall of Fame Teacher. When he retired the next year, the English Department awarded him a plaque with this inscription

To Our
Esteemed Colleague
Thomas Morgan
A Teacher's Teacher
1966 - 1992
Lincoln High School
January 27, 1992

At the last student assembly Tom attended the school choir sang "You Are the Wind Beneath My Wings" as a tribute to him. He was honored to receive these accolades from students and peers at the end of his teaching career.

Part Three
Chess Mentor

Although Tom as the Billy Graham of the bachelors fell off his pedestal, he did not lose his evangelism about chess. He was at his happiest when he could introduce his favorite pastimes to family, friends, and students, hoping to plant the seeds for future pleasures. Tom wanted people to enjoy the delights he found in these activities.

Chess fascinated Tom with its discipline, its challenges, its strategies, its philosophy, its history. He was a student of the game and became a lifelong member of the United States Chess Federation .

A story Tom often told was how the discovery of the New World by Christopher Columbus under the aegis of the Spanish king resulted from a chess match. King Ferdinand of Spain did not want to grant the rank of admiral to Columbus. The offended Columbus decided to leave Spain with his plans for exploration. This news came to the court when the king was playing chess. Queen Isabella wanted to speak for Columbus but did not want to interrupt Ferdinand's game. A courtier, watching the game, knew the queen's intentions and thought she could better influence the king if he was in a good mood at the end of the match with a win, not a loss which seemed imminent. This courtier told the queen a move the king could make to avert a loss. As the king started to make the wrong move, the queen distracted him. He stopped, reviewed the board, made the right move, and not only averted a loss, but produced a win. The queen then spoke on behalf of Columbus. Magnanimous after his chess win, the king agreed to recall Columbus. History hinged on the outcome of a chess match.

The social phase of the game entertained Tom. He spent many hours playing chess with friends who often called him their mentor. In due course, he taught the game to his nephews and godson.

Relishing the challenge of competitive matches, he entered a few local tournaments and did well. He won these awards.

1971   Bayonne, New Jersey, Summer Open, Top Class D, Trophy
1971   Manhattan Novice Chess Open, 1st Place, Trophy and $50
1974   Hudson County, New Jersey, Chess League,
          2nd Place, Trophy
1983   US Chess Federation, Class Tournament,
          1st Place, Postal Chess, Award

Not satisfied with local competition, Tom entered two United States Open Chess Tournaments, one in Atlantic City, the other in Manhattan. The question he posed was how would he fare against players from around the nation and the world? His results in these events placed him about 260 and 270 among the 500 or so entrants. That satisfied him, he did what he wanted, he found the answer to his question. He ranked about midway against national and international competition.

Postal chess gave Tom another forum, one for games played at a leisurely pace with ranked opponents at the same level. The USCF provided the materials, players, ranking, and format. A post card was not as exciting as a live competitor, but the player still had the challenge of the game and maintained an active USCF ranking. Two of his postal opponents were Richard Threlkeld, a CBS-TV reporter, and Cleveland Amory, the writer. The occasional non-chess comments ranged from scribblings in the margins of the post cards to long letters. This correspondence offered interesting insights into his competitors.

The Lincoln High School Chess Club was the highlight of Tom's accomplishments in chess. After personally experiencing the dynamics and excitement of the game, it was natural for an enthusiast like Tom to take it to the next level. Wasn't this a great game for high school youngsters? Tom thought so. Chess would nurture life skills like mental discipline, advance planning, problem solving, creative solutions, patience, perseverance - all attributes that could carry them through their lifetime. Economically, most of the school's students came from the lower class, some from the middle and upper-middle class. Jersey City's population was heavily Catholic and the city had many private Catholic elementary and high schools. That left the public school enrollment mainly with students of color. Lincoln High School drained a neighborhood that was predominantly black and its student body reflected that fact. Jersey City had a Catholic secondary school for boys, St. Peter's Prep, a Jesuit institution, and the elite from the city and county sent their sons there. It had a fine academic reputation. Of course, chess was an extracurricular activity in which the Prep excelled. That was Tom's challenge- not only to have a chess club in Lincoln, but to develop a chess team that could be a presence in the matches around the city, county, and state. Who were these upstarts from a public school like Lincoln to field a chess team? Hah! Not to worry, but in a few years, worry they did.

In the late 1960's Tom started the Chess Club which met once a week-learning, playing, practicing, enjoying themselves. Early on with the club members' approval, Tom instituted a club rating system for the weekly meetings with scores published monthly. This strengthened their play, encouraged competitive spirit, and sharpened them for tournament matches. Soon they were seasoned. To join the county league the players were required to be members of the USCF. The team of five boards played under USCF rules with a clock and had to make 40 moves within 80 minutes. On the first two boards Harry Riff and Leslie Horowitz battled the strength of the county and held their own. The depth of the next three boards: Sam DiFalco, Ronnie Hagood, Kevin Brown, Robert Violante, and Nancy Gross carried the day.

Nancy Gross achieved a first for the Chess Club. She was not intimidated by the male presence in the club and its

Nancy Gross, Hudson County Woman Chess Champion

implied aura of superiority. Undaunted, she competed in match play regularly and became the Hudson County Woman Chess Champion. What a success story!

The brightest day for the club was Feb. 14, 1973, when the New Jersey State Championship Tournament was held in Bayonne. In a field of 66 teams, Lincoln finished fifth. The boards were Harry Riff, Leslie Horowitz, Sam DiFalco, Ron Hagood, and Kevin Brown.

Lincoln High's Chess Club was the only Jersey City public high school, one of five, with a team that consistently ranked just one or two places below St. Peter's Prep, the perennial powerhouse. In fact, in 1972 Lincoln knocked St. Peter's Prep out of the county championship by dealing that team its only loss. The match lasted six hours and ended with a score of 3 ½ to 1 ½. Lincoln High made its presence felt in the Hudson County Chess League.

This was the record of Lincoln's Chess Team.

HUDSON COUNTY CHESS LEAGUE
Lincoln High School Chess Team

	Wins	Losses	Draws	County Final Ranking
1969-70	1	8	1	8th
1970-71	5	5	1	5th
1971-72	10	2	0	3rd
1972-73	6	1	2	3rd
1973-74	8	2	1	2nd

Outstanding Player Awards

1971	Sam DiFalco	8-2
1972	Kevin Brown	11-1 Best fifth board in county
1973	Kevin Brown	Undefeated
1973	Sam DiFalco	Undefeated, untied
	Ron Hagood	Undefeated
	Nancy Gross	Hudson County Woman Chess Champion
1974	Peter Sanders	9-1-1, Best third board in county

The ethnic composition of the Chess Club was a mixture of blacks and whites from various nationalities. These differences - ethnic, economic, racial- did not matter. The game overshadowed all and made them non-factors. The game became the focus of these young players. The Lincoln High School Chess Club became a major force in the league and its members achieved singular honors.

At this time advisors to club activities received no stipends. Tom often came home about 10 PM after ensuring team members got home safely from matches. He used his own car, a Volkswagen, and his own money for snacks to ward off the players' hunger during long competitions. But there is joy in doing what you love and sharing it with young people who find the same joy in that activity. Tom and the members of his chess teams shared that supreme pleasure.

Ron Hagood, Pete Sanders

Lincoln High School Chess Club: standing (L to R) Sam DiFalco, Anthony Kartsounas, Leslie Horowitz, Joseph Greenaway, Wayne Vaughn, Mr. Morgan (Advisor), Robert Violante, Vincent Lopez, Howard Rosen, Joseph Minor; sitting (L to R) Peter Sanders, Nancy Gross, Elsie Pinoliar, Harry Riff

Part Four

Eager Athlete

In his early years Tom's physical activities centered around the need to find an outlet for his youthful energy. Many boys in the neighborhood had this same need. Since solo pursuits were not the order of the day in the Bronx, it was natural that the boys gravitated toward teams. They played in an area circumscribed by streets lined on both sides with parked cars. The surfaces were asphalt in the streets, dirt in the empty lots, cement on the sidewalks. Whatever was there was used. No parks, no grass for them. These were tough Bronx kids.

And tough kids played rough games. Ring-a-leevio was a running game with two sides, usually older boys against younger ones. Each side had any number of players. Whoever showed up took part. They designated a certain place as the "den." The object was to catch all members of the opposition (almost impossible, but no one cared) and put them in the "den." The older runners chased the others, grasped them, yelled, "Ring-a-leevio, coca cola," three times and the victim went to the "den." However, any uncaptured member of the chased team could run to the "den," step into it and yell, "Free all!" The captives scampered from their prison and the chase started all over again. It was really a never-ending game. The fun was in the chase, being chased, and eluding capture. This carefree fun used a great deal of energy, required no equipment or gear, occupied a lot of time, and kept them out of trouble.

Johnny-on-the-pony was different. One team had "Johnny" stand with his back against the wall and a teammate bent toward him grasping his waist. The rest of the team assumed the same bent position and held the waist of the boy ahead of him, thus forming the vague shape of a "pony". Then, all the boys on the opposing side would jump onto the bent backs hoping to dislodge their hold on each other and break the back of the "pony." They left this game with sore muscles. Bruises were badges of honor. Of course, they came home with dirty clothes. The dirtier, the better. No clean clothes for them. That's for sissies!

Every boy in the neighborhood had three shoe boxes: one for marbles, one for bottlecaps, and one for trading cards. Marbles in the first box included aggies, blueys, other colors, and a few clobbalos, the shooters that were larger than the regular marbles. Bottlecaps filled the second box and provided the ammunition for skelly, a game similar to marbles but played only with bottlecaps. A special cap was the shooter for skelly. Cards that were pictures of movie stars, boxers, cowboys, celebrities jammed the third box. The object was to accumulate cards by calling heads or tails when the card was flipped by the owner. If you made the correct call, you won the card from the flipper. Your wrong call resulted in a retained card for the flipper. Your winnings became your trading cards. Tom had a fairly large collection of these cards.

Many boys had their own homemade go-carts. This vehicle had a short plank on two rollers cannibalized from skates and a short wooden crate nailed to one end. Handles projected from the sides of the crate to provide support, steering, and direction. This was usually the first set of "wheels" preceding the bicycle.

And who could forget Slap-ass Johnny? Whenever the gang ran, which was quite often, Johnny, motivated by cowboy movies, always slapped his rump to run faster or so he thought. It never happened.

In the summer Tom and his family spent two weeks at Rockaway Beach where he loved to frolic in the rough wave action of the Atlantic Ocean. He became a strong swimmer. Occasionally, the boys scraped up enough coins to take the subway downtown to Manhattan's Central Park to get to Belvedere Castle. There they became Robin Hood and his Merry Men, scaled the ramparts, swashbuckled around with their makeshift swords to rescue everybody in distress to right some imagined wrong! What fun!

During cold weather they took a potato from any source, placed it in some flame proof container, and built a fire to bake that potato. They called this a Mickey. Tom said it was delicious.

The boys did not need food but nourishment from the camaraderie of friends sharing a pleasant activity. Tom and his friends had a lot of fun, enjoyed their youth, and stored up many memories to relive in their later years.

Ball games were another story. The earlier ones were punchball and stickball, street variations of baseball. To play punchball the boys needed only a spaldeen, a small, hard rubber ball. They hit the ball with their fists, ran the identified bases, and scored when they reached home base. Stickball was more complicated. Not only did the game require a spaldeen but a bat, usually a cut-off broom stick. It was even classier to wrap tape around one end of the broom stick to get a better grip for hot and sweaty hands. This version required a pitcher and usually had more players.

The boys' stickball game on the street moved to stickball in school yards when Tom graduated from high school. Like the other games, this required only a spaldeen and a stick. However, the site was different - a big, fenced in school yard and a wall with a painted box indicating the strike zone. The minimum number on a team was two - a pitcher and a fielder; the maximum was nine. Players located certain spots in the yard as bases. It was at this time that Tom's penchant for numbers appeared. He kept a record of his stickball games as an adult. Tom pitched in most of his games and listed all his statistics: strikes, balls, outs, hits by opponents. This information provided a profile of his game-strengths, weaknesses, what worked, what failed, strengths and weaknesses of hitters. The pay-off came later when the teachers of the high school played stickball regularly. Over the years Tom's record as a pitcher read 22 wins, 0 losses, 35 - 0, and 46 - 0. That winning streak intensified the competition. Everyone wanted to beat Tom and grumbled.

"We have to get Morgan today."

" Morgan's streak has to end."

"Morgan's record is ridiculous."

The inevitable occurred with the sixty third game. When Tom's record reached 62 - 1, the stickball games ended abruptly.

The incentive to continue playing this game was to stop Tom's streak and, when they accomplished that, it was over! No more games after Tom's one defeat. What an effect he had to compel competition!

A basic tenet in Tom's philosophy of life was to drink deeply of life. He was eager to live, eager to try, eager to experience as much of this world as possible. He did not want life to pass him by. He wanted to catch anything of interest and explore it. Even if it turned out to be a one time event, that was all right. He did not want to regret never having tried it. So it was with parachuting. That activity was a test of his daring. Did he have the nerve to jump out of a plane? After one lesson on a Saturday morning, he parachuted the next Saturday. He was able to do it and do it successfully. End of parachuting.

What would be the next adventure? Several times in Myrtle Beach, South Carolina, we passed a field of gliders. Tom went by it once too often. It was there, he saw it, he had to try it. After a brief introduction to gliding by the owner of the operation, the two of them went aloft. The owner was in a small one engine plane and Tom was in a glider trailing behind. At a certain altitude the two airborne vehicles separated. The airplane soared away and the glider with Tom at the controls rode the thermal currents. Some time later Tom brought the glider in for a soft landing on the proper strip without incident! Exhilarating! But, again, once was enough. He tried, succeeded, and satisfied the need to attempt something new. No more gliding.

Glider instructions

Tom had quick- twitch muscles. In high school he ran an eight minute mile and typed a hundred words a minute. In tennis he was very quick at the net, quick at moving to the ball, quick at volleying the ball. However, he was not above using non-athletic tactics to win. Once in a friendly game of singles his opponent was serving aces. On the change over Tom expressed his admiration for the wrist action in those effective serves and analyzed the mechanics of that stroke. Concentrating on the analysis, the opponent did not serve another ace. Another time in a public tournament of doubles, Tom and his partner faced teen-age brothers who were excellent players. For all their youth they were formidable opponents. The older brother was the better player and, unfortunately with the bigger mouth, was constantly criticizing his brother for any unforced error, poor stroke selection, even though they were ahead. In fact, they won the first set. Tom, ever the opportunist, would say on the change overs, "Why is your brother always on your back? He doesn't appreciate how good you are." The younger player started rebuffing the elder's criticism which led to dissension between them. It wasn't too long before their fragile rapport as partners disintegrated and they lost their concentration. Tom and his partner eked out a win by squeaking ahead in the next two sets. According to Tom's law in sports - anything is fair as long as it is not cheating.

In spite of that strategy of getting into the minds of the opponent, Tom was quite an athlete. He reacted quickly and moved as soon as the ball left his opponent's bat or racket. Being ambidextrous, he often amazed the opposition in tennis by stroking a left-handed forehand on a ball hit to his backhand. Most times the surprise factor and his lefty strength produced a winner. One of the best all-round players at our summer camp in New Jersey once commented that Tom was one "helluva" athlete.

Tom's greatest accomplishment in athletics was running the marathon and completing the seven he entered. This was the reasoning that led to distance running in his own words.

"Life truly begins at forty. Looking for something to get me into lighter, better shape for my transition into

middle age, I started a program of light runnning that just seemed to keep building and surprising me. It culminated in the 1979 Boston Marathon which I ran really just to do fifteen miles or so.

Another surprise - I finished it in just under five hours and was able to go dancing afterwards. In 1981 with the knowledge that I could finish it (marathon), I trained seriously and reduced the time by one hour and ten minutes. New York in 1982 was six minutes longer than the second Boston but was twenty one miles into a twenty three mph headwind. In no wind I might have done a 3:40. The ultimate goal is to break 3:30. I train for that now for the Boston 1983 race. Pneumonia knocked me out of it in 1982 before I could start training for it."

Thus, Tom resolved to follow a running program. To achieve his goals he subscribed to a couple of running magazines, changed his diet, and read books by James Fixx and George Sheehan. It was Sheehan who was the main influence in the development of his regimen: exercises before and after each run, runs of two miles five times a week, a run of four miles once a week. Each successive week the distances of the runs increased to a maximum total of 24-26 miles a week. After the long run, he went for a leisurely swim of at least a half hour at the local YMCA. That once-a-week swim eased out any aches or pains and he was ready for the next week's schedule. Never deviating from this routine, he ran whatever the weather conditions: sun, cloud, rain, snow (exception-sleet), whatever the temperatures:85, 60, 25 degrees, whatever the surface: dirt, track, cement, asphalt, cinder (exception-ice), whatever the terrain: beaches, hills, flats.

In early March of 1979 he lost his way on the long run and discovered he had covered seventeen miles, albeit slowly, and was not even winded. That was when he first thought about the Boston Marathon, a run of 26.2 miles, as a remote possibility. Naturally, he tried to make it a reality. We arrived in Boston early April a couple of days before the marathon, usually run on Patriot's Day. Tom and I drove the streets of the run for a few reasons. He wanted to become familiar with the course, to station me at three locations as his support team of one with water and first aid items, and to locate "Heartbreak Hill." This hill was the last of three that were not much higher than those he ran in Livingston, New Jersey, my parents' hometown where he often ran to maintain his training regimen. Runners reach "Heartbreak Hill" about the eighteen or nineteen mile mark of the race when they traditionally can run out of "gas" and "hit the wall." Diet provides the "gas," the stamina. Carbohydrates should make up at least three quarters or more of the tank and proteins make up the rest. If there are no problems, this equation gives the marathoner the energy to complete the series of hills and continue downhill to the flat section and the finish line in Hancock Plaza, Boston. If he or she has used up the carbos before the hills and must use proteins for energy before reaching those three hills about the three quarter mark in the race, the runner is unlikely to run past the third hill, aptly named "Heartbreak Hill." When this happens, the racer won't be able to stand or even put one foot in front of the other. It's as if he or she has run into a wall or has "hit the wall." Tom could not find that hill on our trial drive.

Since Tom was not a registered runner, he had a leisurely, carbohydrate loaded breakfast that included lots of pancakes with syrup and bread before the race. We drove to Hopkinton where the marathon began, arriving about an hour after the start. By then, all the runners with their supporters, race officials with their paraphernalia, media with their equipment had gone. However, the thousands of runners left their mark - their discarded warm-up suits were piled in 8' high mounds that lined both sides of the street for blocks. We learned that the sanitation department would pick up the clothes as trash. Hopkinton was a ghost town; no one was in the streets except Tom and me.

Tom gave me his warm-up suit, not to be discarded, and I gave him a kiss for luck. He started on his journey of self-discovery, another attempt to see what he can achieve, to see how far he can go. Turning his back to me, he walked into a run with an easy stride, elbows held closely to his sides, forearms positioned comfortably at the waist, hands folded slightly into loose fists at chest height. The arm unit moved rhythmically, economically with no unnecessary motions. He was the only racer making his way down the street between mountains of clothes on his way to Boston, 26.2 miles to the east. I watched til his figure got smaller and disappeared into the distance. My heart swelled with pride for his attempt to run this race, a marathon, after running only four months. My eyes filled with tears for his long, lonely journey of self-discovery to test his physical limits.

Now it was time for me to drive to our first rendezvous at the five mile mark where Tom showed up in fine form. He was exuberant. Boston was a runner's town, a marathoner's town. Even though he started the race late, Tom still found some supporters, youngsters and oldsters, lining the road, offering the ubiquitous orange slices, supplying water, gesturing with thumbs up, telling him, "Way to go!" or "You'll make it!" Elated by this unexpected encouragement, he stopped only long enough to tell me of the spectators' enthusiasm before he went into the next leg of the race. The distance to our next meeting was longer, but Tom's spirits never waned. He stopped for a quick "Hello," and continued.   Tom scheduled our last rendezvous about the 20 mile mark of the race close to Boston College. He knew he could run seventeen miles without being too distressed and thought he could run a few more miles. Thus, the calculation that 20 miles was an achievable, realistic goal. Not expecting to run any more miles, Tom planned to get into the car here and we would drive together to the finish line in Boston. But, when he got into the car, he was euphoric and exclaimed, "I'm running to the finish line!" My mouth dropped.

He explained, " A little way back I asked a young man where "Heartbreak Hill" was. The young man said, 'It's behind you, man! It's all downhill the rest of the way!' I started to cry and felt I could finish the race or at least try."

And, so he did, he did both. He tried and finished. Tom ran to the finish line, completing his first marathon, the Boston, his time 4 hrs. 59 min. 36 sec. after he left Hopkinton. He was thrilled as was I.

1979 Tom at the start of the
Boston Marathon,
Hopkinton, Massachusetts

1979 Tom at the finish line,
Boston Marathon, Hancock
Plaza, Boston

Back at the hotel Tom kept to his regimen: cool down exercises and a swim. The dining room was down a short flight of stairs. Holding my hand, he jauntily skipped me down each step. He was on such a high from his marathon accomplishment, floating on a cloud. Of course, we went dancing to continue the celebration. We topped off the evening by having a nightcap at an Irish pub, one of Tom's favorite watering holes. This one, the Black Rose, was recommended by a local. It was filled with a lively, young crowd and had a talented fiddler who performed such a rousing rendition of "The Orange Blossom Special" that he finished with broken strings dangling from his instrument. Truly a perfect ending for a very special day.

Every marathoner should run the Boston race at least once. If at all possible, it should be the runner's first, and he will be hooked on it for life. All Bostonians are fans of the race and many are runners, at least it seemed so during the days preceding this marathon. Their enthusiasm for the event was high, their encouragement for the participants was strong and salutary, capable of putting after-burners in their running shoes. Where else will Wellesley girls pat you on your rump and shout, "Way to go, Gramps!" Tom had a white beard for that race. He seriously thought about turning around there to run past the girls again.

After this first marathon in Boston, Tom completed three more in Beantown, one in Manhattan, one at the Jersey Shore, and one on the Jersey Waterfront. His best time was 3:50:9 for his second one also run in Boston. He was two years older but about one hour and ten minutes faster. You can get better with age.

So many people train for months to attain a goal and never reach it. How utterly frustrating! Plan your work and work your plan. Tom focused on an objective and achieved it with proper training and dieting which led to a successful attempt for running and fitness. Initially, he developed a routine with incremental changes for running and in four months finished his first marathon. With such success he maintained that program and completed six more marathons over the years. In effect, this distance running regimen evolved into a different life style that led to physical fitness, Tom's ultimate goal.

RESULTS OF TOM'S MARATHONS

1979	Boston Marathon	4:59:36
1981	Boston Marathon	3:50:09
1982	New York Marathon	3:58:17
1983	Boston Marathon	3:53:16
1984	New Jersey Shore Marathon	3:51:06
1985	Boston Marathon	3:52:28
1986	New Jersey Waterfront Marathon	3:57:47

1986 Jersey Waterfront Marathon,
Tom with support team members Dorothy and Kivin Chin

1986 Jersey Waterfront Marathon, Tom's cheering section (L to R) Kivin Chin, Tom, Dorothy Chin, Ed Tavss, son Michael Tavss, wife Roberta Tavss

And for the next challenge after a marathon? Yes, Tom entered a triathlon, the 1990 Garden State Tin Man Triathlon that included a half mile swim, a 23 mile bike ride, a ten kilometer run. Again, he was spurred on to try something new, to find out how far he could go, to see if he could finish in good condition with the proper training. His objective as usual was not to win but to finish. The preparation for this event was not as rigorous as for a marathon. He had maintained a regular schedule of running with a long swim at least once a week and had started cycling every week or so. The last was included because Tom liked the advantages of cross-training, using other muscles, expanding his activities. And, of course, once he had reached his goals for the marathons, he had to go to the next step - the triathlon. Now with this event definitely in his sights, the only part he had to train for diligently was longer distances with cycling.

As a novice triathlete, Tom started this event in early June in the third group following the expected winners and experienced competitors. They raced into the water for the swim, the first leg. Finishing the swim in his expected time, Tom nonchalantly strolled up the beach to his support team of my nephew Kivin, his wife Dorothy and son Nicholas, and me who had his clothes and supplies for the cycling, the second leg. Others frantically raced to their bikes with shoes already in place on the pedals and took off in very little time. Tom disappeared into the men's lockers and did not reappear until 30 minutes later, showered, lathered with SPF 30 to protect his fair Irish skin, clothed appropriately for both cycle and run. And, this was a race! His unique distinction in this event was being the last contestant to leave the staging area for cyclists. He had no difficulty locating his bicycle. It was the only one there! Tom was incredibly casual. Again, his aim was not to win this event, his first attempt at a triathlon. He was testing himself, exploring his limits.

1990 Garden State Tin Man Triathlon: Nicholas Chin, second generation for Tom's support team, Ruth, Tom, the triathlete

Although Tom was the last person to start the bicycle leg, he was not the last to finish it. Since this was the untested part of the triathlon on an uncharted course, he overestimated his time. Not only did he complete it sooner than predicted, but a few other cyclists came in after him. And even with that loss of 30 minutes at the start of the cycling, he began the 10K run, the third leg of the race, much earlier than expected. After we secured his bicycle in the staging area for the run, we ambled over to the streets along the chute leading to the finish line, found a comfortable spot, and plunked ourselves down to wait, an inevitable part of the support team's day. Knowing that Tom was fairly consistent with his running time, I guesstimated when he would finish. I started looking for him before the others did. Peering down the street far from the finish line, I spotted Tom's figure; he looked about three to four feet tall from that distance. Everyone said it could not be Tom; it was too early. Unequivocally, I maintained it was Tom. His posture, his gait, his stride, his arms, his fists, I would recognize him anywhere. As the figure neared, his features became clearer. We all cheered and shouted his name so he could locate us. When he heard , looked, and spotted us, he pumped his right arm into the air and crossed the finish line at 2:58:06 after the start of the contest. Tom finished his first and last triathlon, just wanting to see if he could do it, and he did. He was quietly thrilled with his latest athletic feat. It was a noble effort, a job well done.

 Next, there was dancing. True to form, Tom made this another physical activity. When in high school, he did what most fellows his age did. They attended the school dances and were the male wall flowers. Cloaked in their assumed mantle of male arrogance and superiority which we now know really disguised their inadequacy in dancing, they would stand against the wall, look over the scene, appraise the girls, and regard them as unworthy of their attention. Consequently, they never danced.

On the other hand, we girls were smart enough to know what their attitude was and would not let that ruin our evening. We proceeded to dance to every tune without them, learned how to do every kind of dance, and enjoyed ourselves. If we waited for the boys to ask, we would never dance. In post-high school years Tom's work with the Treasury Department left him little time for this particular leisure activity about which he knew nothing anyway. When he started college with night classes after work, he certainly had no time for much of anything.

After we were married, I tried constantly to get Tom on the dance floor, to no avail. The catalyst that led him to dance was the music in a nearby bistro, the Cornerstone in Metuchen, New Jersey, which featured the best traditional jazz in the state. As we were both jazz fans, we became regulars there, and that fine music finally got Tom's toes tapping. Fortunately, some good dancers showed that it was fun to trip the light fantastic. He finally found the courage to step onto the darkened dance floor and we danced in a corner. He found that all he had to do was move to the beat, to the rhythm of the music. A Eureka moment - he tried it and liked it! After that it was easy to get him on the dance floor, especially with the music he liked, and the music he liked to dance to was fast. Later, his favorite dance was the one or two step, a physical, energetic one, of course. Spontaneity and creativity marked his dancing because he knew no steps. He just improvised, always to the beat. He threw in herky-jerky moves, duck waddles, hippity-hops, patty-cake handslaps that delighted onlookers. Not knowing what he was going to do next, I did double time to fall in with his steps and just followed his lead. Most times we were out of breath when we finished the quick steppers. Our footwork, such as it was, and the fun we had so impressed some viewers that they felt compelled to ask us where we took lessons. We answered vaguely, smiled our thanks for their kind words, and walked away, not wanting to disillusion our admirers.

A few times as we left the dance floor, there was a smattering of applause; people smiled at us and made flattering comments about our dancing. When we reached our table, Tom asked me, "Are we that good?" My response, "To them we are. Let's leave it at that and enjoy the moment."

At times Tom wanted to dance when I didn't! What a turnaround! I created a dancing Frankenstein!

Part Five
Eveready Fisherman

One of Tom's favorite authors was Ernest Hemingway. When Tom sported a heavy beard, white in his later years, many people remarked that he looked like Hemingway. Naturally, Tom was flattered. The Hemingway book he enjoyed most was <u>The Old Man and the Sea</u> not only because Tom himself was an avid fisherman but because of the old man's philosophy, his struggle and relationship to the sea, to the fish, and to the young friend. Many times Tom experienced those long hours with a rod in his hand hoping a fish would take the bait, then struggle, fighting for its life. Some times Tom won, some times the fish won. Even when he came home empty-handed and disappointed, he never thought it was a waste of time. It was the way of life on the sea. He realized the fish were not in the waters looking for a fisherman's bait. They were there searching for food to survive. It was a stroke of luck accompanied by some skill if the recreational fisherman caught an occasional fish and, if he didn't, there was always another day. Fortunately, fishing was not his livelihood.

Fishing was the leisure activity Tom enjoyed the most. The night before a fishing trip in New Jersey he spent hours lining up all the necessities, awakened before dawn to put all the gear into the car, drive about two hours south on the Garden State Parkway to the shore towns of Brielle or Point Pleasant, eat a quick breakfast, and then board a headboat, preferably, one of Bogan's. He always took his big cooler carrying his lunch and the obligatory beers for the day. In the natural course of events, these contents were gradually consumed, and the cooler became empty, ready to hold his big catch of fish for the ride home. A fisherman is the eternal optimist. More often than not he came home with no or few fish, but he had some experiences worth recounting.

Tom had heard stories of the big spring mackerel run off the

Jersey shore and the huge numbers caught in one outing. He went a few times and was disappointed. But persistence pays off. On a fine April day he came home from fishing and rang the doorbell. I wondered why he didn't use his key. He wanted to astound me and he certainly did. I opened the door for him and there he stood like Santa Claus, grinning from ear to ear. Slung over his shoulder was a big burlap bag filled to bursting with something.

I asked, "What in heaven's name do you have in that bag?"

"One hundred mackerel!" he proudly announced.

"What are you going to do with a hundred mackerel?" was my shocked exclamation.

"Scale them, gut them, pack them, and give them away," was the fisherman's reply.

He would not give away unscaled, ungutted fish, heaven forbid! He thought he was a fishmonger. But I was not a happy fishmonger's wife that late afternoon with scales flying from the two of us working in a small sink in a small kitchen in a small three room apartment. A few hours later halfway through the job, I groused and grumbled the only ultimatum I ever made in our marriage.

"Don't ever come into our home to scale or clean fish again!"

And he never did. We were finding fish scales all over the kitchen months after his record catch. But many friends and neighbors happily accepted fresh, cleaned mackerel for their dinner.

Soon after we relocated to a new home which, fortunately, had a back yard large enough for Tom to cultivate a vegetable patch. Tom did the fish cleaning in this area and used the fish remains as fertilizer. This led to great results with his vegetable garden, particularly for the tomatoes.

Every social activity was planned with something special to add fun. Once Tom arranged a night of bluefishing with Ed, his best friend and fishing buddy, and Jim who was on his first fishing trip with Tom. Yes, Tom felt obliged to make this a memorable event for Jim. Tom bought a toy duck, filled it with sand, and planned to attach it to Jim's line. This happened to be a slow night for fishing which made it easy for co-conspirator Ed to get Jim to the inside cabin for beer and allow Tom to put the duck on Jim's line, a difficult job to do. Needing more time, Tom managed to give Ed the high sign, and Jim didn't need much persuasion to have another beer. When they came back from the beers, Jim saw a deep bend in his pole and exclaimed, "I must have a huge fish on that line. Maybe it'll be the pool fish!" Since few men were catching fish, Jim's announcement created a stir and a crowd gathered offering shouts of advice and encouragement about bringing in the "big one." After some feverish exertion, the "monster" finally broke the surface of the water. The laughter roared through the boat and traveled over the water as Jim reeled in a rubber duck. Jim was a good sport and enjoyed telling his "fish story" about how he won the "pool duck."

A gregarious soul , Tom wanted to share activities he enjoyed with people he liked. Usually asking friends and family members to join him on fishing trips, he also made a special effort to take many of his nephews on their first fishing expeditions. Helping others to have fun with a new experience was one of the joys in Tom's life.

After many attempts Tom finally organized a daytime fishing excursion with several of his male friends. As happenstance would have it, most of the wannabe fishermen were Irish, and as Tom would have it, a few were first timers. His goal was camaraderie set in a productive atmosphere- catching fish for food and having fun. And, in fact, they did, have too much fun, that is.

Jeannette O'Rourke, wife of one of the novice fishermen, called me about five o'clock to learn when to expect her husband Willie to get home from this male bonding experience.

"It's difficult to set a time," I replied, "because if few fish are caught, the captain of the boat would stay out to sea longer to find fish and return to port with happy customers. Anyway," I continued unfortunately, "Tom always calls me when he disembarks and gives me an ETA (expected time of arrival) . I'll call you as soon as Tom does."

Nothing assuaged Jeannette's fears. She called me every half hour, managing to phone a few other wives who in turn called me. After reassuring all the others, I began to have misgivings, too. A while later Jeannette told me about her last call - to the Coast Guard. When the Coast Guardman heard her concern about the safety of her husband, he informed her that no fishing vessel issued distress calls that day, and all licensed boats were required to have radios. He assured her that in all likelihood at that very moment, the location of her husband was in the bar closest to the docks and there the men were exchanging stories and playing gamesmanship of some kind. Whatever the case, all the men were safely ashore.

Around nine that evening Roberta Tavss, wife of the only non-Irishman in this group, heard from her husband Ed. He explained that as soon as the men disembarked and put away their catch, they headed to the nearest bar as predicted by the Coast Guard. It must be some kind of time-honored piscatorial excursion ritual. As they entered the watering hole, some inspired mischief-maker announced that the first one to call his wife was a wimp! The gauntlet was thrown. Realizing that they had fun long enough about not calling home to reassure the wives, Ed was the first to come to his senses and phone his wife alerting her that all was well. However, he did make the call, unbeknownst to the others of course, on the way to the rest room. Roberta kindly made the calls to us waiting at home.

I know these men loved and respected their wives, but males are transformed when gathered in such groups and challenges are tossed around to see who blinks first. It's a macho thing. Some of the men taught at the same school. That mandated this silence could not be broken by any of them; otherwise, horrific, endless teasing would resound through the school for a very long time. These men's lips were sealed.

Such enthusiasm as Tom had for fishing was interesting and long lasting. Eventually it had to reach out to me. Although my fishing trips were rare, there were enough to frustrate me and dampen any desire to do this frequently. One hot summer Tom had gone at night for bluefish a few times and came home with quite a few fish. Freshly caught bluefish is delicious, as is any fish just caught. He asked me to accompany him, but I usually declined. During one long hot spell in August, I relented and decided to join Tom for the cool evening on the Atlantic waters and lovely seascapes seen on the ride out to the fishing grounds. Those pleasant experiences would make up for returning without any blues. We boarded a headboat that Tom had used a few times that summer and, recognized as a regular, the mates chatted with him. Always trying to arouse interest in the routine, Tom bet one of the mates that I would catch at least five blues this trip. Blues are reputed to be among the fiercest fighters for their size on the Jersey coast. The mate squinted at me, approximated my size: five feet high, 105 pounds. He thought it was a safe bet.

"How much ?" he asked.

"One dollar and seventy two cents," Tom answered.

They shook hands.

When the captain of a headboat reaches the fishing ground, he turns off the engines and blows a horn - the signal for the fishermen to drop their baited hooks into the water. The captain does not want trailing lines to be caught in his propellers. This night we arrived at the grounds after an hour's ride and the entire visible surface of the ocean, illuminated by the boat's huge spotlights, shimmered with silvery streaks - blues! Big schools of blues! The eager fishermen didn't wait for the captain's signal. Everyone including Tom and me dropped a line before the captain could blow his horn.

After a few minutes I told Tom my hook was caught between rocks or some thing attached to the boat. He calmly told me, "You have a blue on your line."

"No, no," said I, the novice fisherwoman. "I keep pulling my line, and it's taut, no movement."

We both maintained our opposite positions. Finally, turning to him to emphasize my point, I unconsciously loosened my grip on the pole slightly; the fish felt the relaxed tension on the line, seized this opportunity to escape, and made a dash for freedom.

My line with the bluefish at one end sang as it rapidly ran out from the reel.

I cried out, "I have a fish!" Tom rolled his eyes, raised his eyebrows, and gave me an "I told you so" look. But he graciously helped me dance over and under the lines of the nearby fishermen as the blue swam away struggling to free itself from the hook. Somehow I held on, brought in a tired fish on my taut line, lifted it above the water's surface for the mate's gaff - an eighteen inch blue. Not only did I catch a blue, but I got it before Tom caught his. With his competitive spirit he always added a wrinkle to spice the action - who would catch the first fish, catch the largest, catch the most. No prizes for the distinction, just meeting the challenge and just beating Tom was the ultimate satisfaction for me. I must admit that Tom had a handicap this trip - me. He took care of all the dirty work that went with this activity. I had none of it. I just had to hold the pole and bring in the fish.

That night I caught nine blues in about two hours. It might not sound like much, but I was exhausted and stopped fishing. Catching this size bluefish is not easy. Tom snagged fifteen in about three hours and would have caught more but he had to help me with mine. Not only did he bait my hook, but he also unhooked all my fish. Unhooking an eighteen or nineteen inch blue was not exactly something I preferred to do. Fishermen have been known to lose fingertips snapped off by a vicious blue.

When we disembarked, Tom had to complete his financial transaction with the mate who was astonished to learn the number of blues I caught. But honor among fishermen, he took Tom's word, paid off the bet, $1.72. Tom was very happy. The amount of money wasn't important, winning was. And we both had a pretty good catch of fish which meant a pretty good supply of food. What could be better? It was a good night, all around.

When a fisherman goes out for a day on a headboat, he always harbors the hope of catching the "pool" fish, the biggest fish caught that day. As the men and women board the boat, each contributes a few dollars to build a "pool" of money to reward the person who is lucky enough to get the biggest fish that trip. As often as Tom went out on headboats, he never came home with the "pool" money. Once he arranged a first-time-fishing-together outing with his father and, yes, his father won the "pool" that day. Beginner's luck or the luck of the Irish. But on one warm April day in 2000 Tom and Nicholas, his godson, boarded the Miss Virginia, a headboat out of Port Richey, to try their luck in the Gulf of Mexico. They returned about four o'clock and the pool-fish-bettors brought out their catches for the mates to check for the "pool" fish. Using a simple balance for the weigh-in, the mate hung a good sized fish on one side with another fish on the other side. The one that dipped lower was the heavier fish. Tom's fish was the third or fourth to be weighed and proved to be the fish to beat. The mates tried a few others against Tom's, but none was heavier. So, Tom finally brought in the "pool" fish. He won $90. Since Tom and Nicholas went out together, Tom paid for each to enter the pool with the agreement that whoever won the pool would split the winnings between them. As luck would have it, one of them did catch the biggest fish, and each came back with $45. A very good day of fishing out on the gulf.

The main purpose of fishing in Tom's view was the sport, the challenge, man versus fish. Man did everything possible to lure the fish to his bait, set the hook, bring in the fish. And the fish did everything possible to get off the hook, to survive. Tom also believed that the fish caught had to be eaten, not wasted. If you did not plan to eat it, you released it. For all that thinking, Tom did entertain thoughts of catching one trophy fish. His ideal specimen was the sailfish. Its large dorsal fin looking like a sail made it a desirable trophy and you had to look for it in warm waters. The closest warm water for us in New Jersey was the Gulf Stream off Cape Hatteras, North Carolina. This stream with a width comparable to a river hugs the eastern coast of Florida and flows north until it hits Cape Hatteras where it turns eastward across the Atlantic Ocean to the next land mass - the southwestern shore of England.

Tom's favorite spot to get the "big" fish was Oregon Inlet near Cape Hatteras. After a few years of fishing excursions to this inlet, he still had no trophy. He always came back to port with fish-some good sizes in tuna, the occasional blue, and other small varieties, but the "big" one always eluded him. He never even had one bite. Early one summer he had another unsuccessful attempt at Oregon Inlet to get something to mount on his wall. That's when he decided to book a charter boat that took only four fishermen for late August, early September. No more headboats. Now was the time for the big show.

The week before Labor Day 1978 the charter agent from Oregon Inlet called Tom about a boat available for a trip the Saturday after Labor Day, but no one else was registered for this day. Without hesitation Tom booked it. His reasons were he wanted to do this, he was free, here was his chance. Also, with four men on board the procedure to determine the order of fighting the hooked fish was the pulling of straws. If he were the fourth man, he might not even have a chance for a fish. What were the chances of four fish being hooked in one day? Being the only one on board, he had the chance at the first bite, the second bite, as many bites that took place. One can understand anybody's eagerness to board a charter as the only fisherman aboard - exclusive albeit expensive. I went along for the ride.

We made the necessary preparations and left after school on Friday, drove through the night, and arrived at Oregon Inlet in time for a quick breakfast, and boarded the "Fish-N-Fool" about nine next morning. The first mate and captain greeted us. The mate was a blond, sun-tanned young man in shorts. The captain had brown hair streaked with gray atop a medium-tanned face with wrinkles and wore a long-sleeved shirt and long pants. After the captain mumbled what I thought was a greeting, he shook our hands and scrambled up the ladder to the bridge. He had the thickest drawl I ever heard and, if he had conversed with us, we would have needed an interpreter even for a monosyllabic word. We learned he came from the western mountains of North Carolina; how does a mountaineer get so knowledgeable about the denizens of the deep seas to make a living out of it? Interesting.

However, this captain was no fishing fool. While we were

sleeping, he steered eastward and in an hour reached the Gulf Stream about forty miles from shore. We were awakened by the silence when the roar of the engines subsided as they shifted to idle. It was quite a sight - the long outriggers slowly lowered into position, one on each side, the long lines from the outriggers trailed steadily aft; the captain started trolling, keeping the lines steady as they sliced through the water. This was show time, hopefully.

About fifteen minutes later, it was! We heard a garbled shout from the bridge. The mate told us later that sound from the captain was the word, "Fish!" Could have fooled me. This was it! We saw one of the lines racing out, heard it whirring out. Tom jumped into the single fighting chair, faced stern, strapped himself in while the mate took the pole from the outrigger and placed it in the holder between Tom's legs. The fish ran out quite a distance. I looked up at the captain, half turned in his seat. He had his right hand on the wheel and his left hand on a railing to keep himself steady. In this position he maintained the proper speed and direction of the boat while he never took his eyes off Tom fighting in the chair and the fish fighting in the water. The captain's role was crucial to help Tom bring in the fish. Alert to the reactions of the fish, the captain had to maneuver the boat to keep the line straight between the fisherman's pole and the fish no matter what evasive actions the fish took. Also, he wanted Tom, his client, to capture his trophy fish so he could build his reputation as a good captain. The white marlin took out line for several more minutes and could not dislodge the hook. All this while Tom played the fish perfectly, keeping the line taut and developing a rhythm of letting out the line, reeling it in, lowering the pole, raising it high, no variations. Some time later the fish changed tactics and decided to sound. When that happened, the mate noted that was a typical action for a male. Can you believe a macho quality even among the Pisces? The male goes down as far as he can trying to overpower his opponent at the other end of the line and escape somehow. The earlier run must have tired Mr. White Marlin because in a short while Tom had his catch. All told, it was about a 30 minute fight to bring the marlin alongside the boat. The mate asked Tom if he wanted to mount the fish.

"Of course," was the reply. What other reply was possible? The mate carefully gaffed it and brought it aboard. Tom caught his trophy that day- a seven foot, 67 pound white marlin. At long last! It's been mounted on a wall in our home ever since.

But, now my story - same scene, same setting, different cast of characters with a slight variation on the theme. About half an hour after Tom's catch, that same garbled shout came from above. We both knew what it meant this time.

Tom and the mate faced me and said, "Your turn in the chair!"

"Who, me!" I said, bug-eyed.

"Yes, I caught mine, now you catch yours!" Tom quickly answered.

Very reluctantly I seated myself in the chair; Tom strapped me in, always helping me.

The mate placed the pole in the holder and gave me instructions about keeping the pole up and the tension of the line tight, reeling line in, letting line out, getting a rhythm. Meanwhile I'm thinking, "Matey, you've got to be kidding!" Tom knelt beside me on the left, the mate likewise on the right. All the while the line was singing out from the reel when about three football fields away I saw a magnificent athletic feat - a fish, my fish with my hook in its mouth, breached the surface of the water, exposed its entire body vertically in the air, wiggled frantically for a few seconds trying to shake loose the hook, then plunged back into the water. The mate told us this was characteristic of female white marlins. This lady made a couple more marvelous jumps, each was an awesome sight. Imagine the energy it took to propel a seven foot long body up from the depths of the water to expose its entire length well above the water and wiggle in the air a few times. That was a fight!

After some 20 minutes in the fighting chair struggling with this female marlin, I had no energy left and could not continue the fight at my end of the fishing line. I was literally "at the end of my line." I was ready to concede the contest to the piscatorial lady. Tom and the mate encouraged me to go on.

The mate exclaimed, "We have a client who's been trying nineteen years, and he's never even had a bite. This is your first trip and you're going to pull in a marlin!" Wearily, I stayed in the chair.

Because I had to reel it in to call it my catch, Tom and the mate decided I should use two hands for the reel while they held the rod for me. The marlin was tired after those jumps, but she was far away from the boat, and it was a long, tough pull for me. The team position won my fight, an exhausting but exciting one. That lady had me in the fighting chair about 45 minutes. I still have four faint scars from the slight gashes above my left wrist from using two hands for that big reel used to bring in Mrs. Marlin that long distance.

As the mate pulled in my marlin ready to gaff her, he asked me the same question about keeping it; guess it's routine. I declined; one seven foot marlin in a house is enough. He released the fish. The captain registered the event with the state tourist agency which issued a certificate of my successful catch and subsequent release. I often wondered if this female marlin was seeking her mate who had wandered off because the two were caught within 30 - 40 minutes of each other.

Tom got his first catch after seven years and I brought in my first catch on my first outing. It's mostly luck and partly skill or having a lot of help, probably a combination of all three.

Oregon Inlet is an interesting sight around four in the afternoon when all the boats return in a line as if on parade. The boats fly flags to signal their trophy catches to all who wait either to welcome home the fishermen or to buy fresh fish at good prices. Very little food is as tasty as fresh fish. The flags have the color and the shape of the fish that have been captured. If the figure of the fish is right side up, it's on board. If the figure is upside down, it's been released. That day the "Fish-N-Fool" flew two blue flags with white marlins: one marlin was right side up, Tom's; the other was upside down, mine. The knowledgeable docksiders came over to the "Fish-N-Fool" as it pulled into its mooring to see the marlin and to congratulate us, an exciting event for Tom and me. We still have those flags and treasure them as mementoes for "his " and "hers" catches.

This was an expensive fishing expedition when you added the costs of the trip, the charter, the taxidermy, the shipping, but seeing that mounted fish for the rest of your life is satisfaction supreme.

Off Oregon Inlet, North Carolina, Tom, aboard the "Fish-N-Fool" flying the two flags for the fish we hooked

Displaying the white marlin

The white marlin mounted on the wall of our Port Richey home

Another different kind of Pisces Tom wanted to catch was the bonefish, reputedly one of the quickest and most elusive fish in warm waters. The closest bonefish were in the waters off the shores of Abaco, the northernmost island of the Bahamas about an hour's flight due east of Fort Lauderdale, Florida. We booked a room at the Walker's Cay Hotel and Marina in Abaco to catch this unusual specimen, planning to arrive on Sunday, August 23, 1992. Does this date sound familiar? We drove to Newark Airport in New Jersey arriving mid-morning, left our car in the self-parking facility, and checked in for our flight to Abaco with a stopover in Fort Lauderdale. Blithely, we boarded the first leg of our flight on time unaware that a half an hour earlier while we were still in Newark a Walker's Cay Hotel agent called our home to cancel our reservations because a hurricane named Andrew was expected to wreak havoc on the island. By the time we landed in Fort Lauderdale the pilot had informed us of the weather and conditions in the area. Our flight was among the last permitted to land. No more planes in or out. Everything was shut down, a major evacuation was taking place, Interstate 95 was clogged with vehicles traveling north at a snail's pace to get out of harm's way. We were in a quandary since we had no reservations in Fort Lauderdale. Luckily, we found a Good Sam cabbie who was willing to drive us around until we could find a room about 40 minutes later at a Holiday Inn in Fort Lauderdale farther away from the shore. Tom tipped the cabbie handsomely.

Everything said about a powerful hurricane is true. Even though the eye of the storm was 100 miles south of us, the winds well over a 100 mph sounded like a thundering train roaring down the street. The management of the motel was organized and informed guests of safety measures: stay away from windows, draw drapes across them, take refuge in the central core of the building, primarily the bathroom. We were mesmerized with the TV coverage and anxiously watched til dawn when Andrew said, "Good bye," and we vehemently replied, "Good riddance!"

The storm lasted several hours and left with no injuries and little damage in the motel. However, there was no electricity.

But the hotel planned properly for this kind of emergency; the Holiday Inn had a generator and generously provided guests with a simple supper that evening and a continental breakfast the next morning gratis. When we walked around the area after breakfast, the surroundings looked like a war torn area with many downed trees and power lines. The cement block buildings remained intact but smaller structures revealed damaged roofs. Debris was scattered all over the walks and streets. Businesses were closed, roads were empty, very few humans were in sight.

The devastation wrought by Hurricane Andrew as it raged through Fort Lauderdale emphasized the raw, uncontrollable power of Mother Nature. How insignificant is man.

Man proposes. Nature disposes. We planned a bonefishing weekend in Abaco and Nature, courtesy of Hurricane Andrew, canceled that fishing trip.

In June of 1993 we rebooked our trip to Abaco. It was a beautiful little island still in an undeveloped state with its primary focus of providing simple pleasures and simple enjoyments for its guests. Because there were few indications of the passage of Hurricane Andrew through the island about a year earlier, the tourist was able to concentrate on the main attraction of Abaco - fishing. The hotel offered clean, plain rooms, but with no telephones, no televisions, no radios. The hotel had a nice restaurant that served good meals and would even cook your catch for you.

Tom went to the booking agent to check for available services and was lucky enough to find a guide whose client had canceled for the day and was free for an afternoon of fishing. He gladly offered his time and Tom just as gladly accepted it. It was a serendipitous afternoon for both guide and fisherman.

Our expert, who was from Islamorada in the Florida Keys, settled us in a flat bottomed skiff specifically designed for shallow waters and stowed all the necessary gear. While motoring to the fishing grounds, he gave us a quick run down on fly fishing, the technique used to catch bonefish. Tom had read up on this method. I was clueless. Tom was confident, I was game - for fish, ready to try my hand at anything; after all, I reeled in a seven foot white marlin, albeit with help. I wasn't embarrassed to announce that fact.

When we approached the flats with the clear almost transparent water, the guide cut the motor, put on what looked like soft slippers, and climbed about seven feet up onto the poling platform.

This height was a great vantage point to spot fish. He advised us to be quiet as he poled silently, slowly to the area where he thought we would find fish.

With bonefish the angler has to be silent, stealthy in his approach and exacting, delicate in his cast. When bonefish get to their feeding grounds in shallow waters, they know they are vulnerable and are acutely aware of their surroundings. Thus, they are easily startled, "spooked." The fisherman has to cast his hook to let it gently drop upon the water as if it were a natural event, and it can't be too close because the fish will make a mad dash away from this potential danger. Then, if the cast is perfectly placed for a hungry fish to take the hook, the angler will experience the legendary run of the bonefish, one of the fastest, strongest by a fish in shallow water. The bonefish is known to make a first run of 100 yards and a second of almost the same distance in its struggle to escape. They don't give up easily or quickly even with all that energy expended after being hooked.

My attempts at catching a bonefish were futile since I kept developing bird's nests on my line. Tom, however, had better luck. He made the proper cast and successfully hooked a bonefish. After it gave Tom the sensations of experiencing that legendary first long run, this bonefish never regained enough strength for that second dash. Noticing the different tension on the line, Tom started reeling in the fish which was quite a distance away and still struggling to dislodge the hook. Not long after, the guide noticed a triangular fin in the vicinity. A small shark, probably attracted by a fish in distress, was stalking Tom's fish. The poor fish was caught between the devil (Tom) and a denizen (the shark) of the shallow, clear waters. The shark beat Tom to his catch. When the fish was about 100 feet from the boat, the shark sensed it was time to make his move. Tom immediately felt the lessened tension on the line and knew the reason - the shark was swimming away from his line with its meal. He reeled his line in to see what his bonefish looked like. At the end of his line he had a bonefish head with a few inches of body below the gills. The guide estimated the fish to be about sixteen inches long. Tom hooked a bonefish only to have a shark help himself to two thirds of it, generously leaving one third to the helpless fisherman. That's the reality of the life of a fisherman. Tom did not hook another bonefish that weekend.

To prepare for a fishing trip in New Jersey was a major project: gather gear the previous night, rise before the sun, drive a long distance to the headboat, ride a long distance on the boat to the fishing grounds. To prepare for fishing from our canalside home in Port Richey, Florida, was no hassle. Tom had his gear ready to go in the game room off the backyard about 35 feet from the canal, his bait frozen in small packets for easy thawing in the canal, his cooler on the backyard dock. The time lapse between deciding to fish and putting a line in the canal took less than fifteen minutes. What a difference!

His easiest catch was a 40" snook. One winter during a cold spell Tom headed to his concert band practice with his clarinet case in one hand and his music folder in the other. As was his wont, he perambulated the perimeter of the house which included the sea wall and the dock and peered into the water just in case he saw something interesting. Well, this night he did. He saw the dim shape of a fish, motionless, lifeless under the dock. He presumed it was a fish that sought the warmer waters of these canals about a mile from the gulf and died. Curious, he put his music and instrument down, and ran to the shed for the net. He lay down on the dock to get the net under the fish. As soon as he tried to scoop it up, the fish moved. It was alive! It struggled to get out of the net. But Tom persisted and got it into the net. The fish had little energy, obviously, and Tom wasn't going to let this one get away. Nobody would believe this story. Luckily, the cooler was on the dock. That's where the fish went into several inches of sea water from the canal. Too long to lie flat, its fin curved up one side of the cooler. Tom ran back to the house to tell me of his great "catch" and charged me with the task of guarding this snook from predators until he got back from practice.

The fish was safe and still alive that night when Tom returned. Early the next morning he took a picture to back up his fish tale before he cleaned, gutted, and fileted it. This snook provided many delicious dinners for the two of us.

Tom bragged about how easy it was to catch fish in our canal. No rod, no reel, no bait, no hook, just walk to the dock in your backyard and catch a 40" snook. Oh, all right, he did need a net.

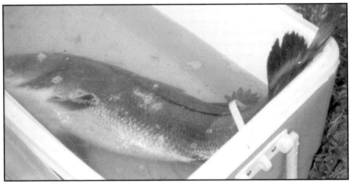

Snook in 36" cooler

A boat was always in Tom's dreams. It was an important part of the recreation equation: boat + fishing = ease. With your own vessel you go at your convenience, go to any destination within reason or limits. And he did not want just any boat. With his research he concluded the ideal vessel was a Grady-White Angler, a reliable, sturdy fishing boat with a good reputation. From this Grady-White you could fish port, starboard, fore, and aft.

The dream boat appeared, a used Grady-White for several thousand dollars. Tom did not want to pull that amount of money from our savings and decided to try his luck in Atlantic City. We went to Harrah's, our favorite casino, and followed our usual routine: dine leisurely, gamble separately each with our own poke, rendezvous at the bar prior to going home. I played the slots exclusively while Tom checked out black jack, craps, and roulette with a $200 poke that he hoped to parlay into a substantial sum toward the purchase of the boat.

After I lost my poke in less than an hour, which really wasn't too bad, I sat at a table in the lounge, nursed a drink, and read my book. When Tom came to the table, I knew he had placed his bet. My first feeling was ambivalence-I wanted to know the outcome; I didn't want to know the outcome. Happy news? Unhappy news? This was so important to Tom. He would be so disappointed with a loss. My heart would ache. It wasn't just the money, it was his boat, his dream. I gazed at him silently, a questioning look with one eyebrow raised slightly. He calmly reached to the inner chest pocket of his sport jacket, pulled out some money, and put it on the table, all this action without expression, flamboyance. I breathed a bit easier, at least it wasn't a total loss. Still not a word out of him.

He forced me to ask, "How much?"

Tom had a flair for the dramatic. He paused, stared at me intently, and quietly answered, mouthing, "$3,200.00!"

My eyes widened and, while they stayed that way, he told me how he did it. He planned to bet on roulette and just take colors, black or red, which was safer than betting numbers 1-36. Strolling around the tables, he scanned the action. He stopped at one table, watched the betting for several minutes, and tried to detect any inkling of a pattern. Unable to get any clues, he finally decided to jump into the action anyway and landed on his feet. Tom parlayed that $200 to $3,200! He let the $200 ride on four successive bets on color. He stopped at $3,200, cashed in his chips, and met me at the bar. How very lucky he was.

We gave a little money back to Harrah's, largesse oblige. Tom bought me a celebratory drink and we left. He was the designated driver. The winnings paid for half the cost of the boat.

After Tom purchased the boat, the next task was to name it. In one respect Tom was not unique. He wanted to name it for me,

Ruth. But Ruth was too prosaic for Tom. Imagine a boat named "Ruth." He had to do it differently, with panache. In this respect he was unique in devising a name for the boat that alluded to me. He knew my parents' ethnic linguistic idiosyncrasy. Unable to pronounce the initial consonant "r" in my name, they substituted "l" for "r." Consequently, their version of my American name was Lutie for Ruthie. Since Tom used the betting money to pay for half the boat, he combined Lutie with loot and coined the name Loo't. Pronounced in two syllables, it is loo-ty; in one syllable, it is loot. He painted LOO'T on the stern of the Grady-White. That was original.

Tom had his power boat, the "LOO'T," and some years later I had my twelve foot aluminum rowboat, the "LOO'T II." We became a two-boat family.

Tom prepared for boating as he did with fishing and running. He never went into an activity as a dilettante. He researched boat ownership carefully and thoroughly by reading periodicals and any size publication. Of course, he bought C.F. Chapman's <u>Piloting, Seamanship, and Small Boat Handling</u>, the boat owner's Bible, and read it cover to cover, annotated and underlined extensively. He also took the United States Coast Guard course in safety and received the certificate of satisfactory completion.

The boat was primarily for fishing, a working boat. But Tom had a deep respect for the ocean, recognizing its dangers and his responsibilities that accompanied the pleasure and pride of boat ownership. After the "LOO'T" took its rightful place next to our two door Nissan in the driveway, Tom purchased safety vests, "Mae Wests." Every first time rider in the "LOO'T" had a safety drill: he or she got a vest from its storage spot, put it on, strapped it properly, and returned it to storage. At this time, Tom spoke briefly about other necessary information for a safe yet fun fishing trip. He wanted to bring home every passenger and the boat in good condition.

All of our family and friends lived in land-locked areas. True to form, Tom wanted them to enjoy the experience that waterside living offered from the canal by our home in Port Richey. He couldn't have all our guests ride in his Grady-White because the boat could only get out at high tide. But he guaranteed all would catch fish. This was not an idle boast. To make good on his promise, Tom put bait in the water by our dock about an hour before our guests arrived. The chum lured the fish to our area. Inevitably, anyone who dropped a line with bait into the canal would catch a fish- the reliable catfish we fondly dubbed Charley Catfish. He or another in his family always showed up and delighted the person at the other end of the line. Everyone caught a fish as predicted. Tom dedicated himself to entertaining all who honored us with a visit to our home.

The "LOO'T" docked in the canal beside our Port Richey home

Part Six
Creative Humorist

Tom was insecure when meeting new people socially. He needed a little support and encouragement before his personality would blossom. On our way to a party where he didn't know too many of the other guests, he would ask, "What am I going to say for a couple of hours?" I suggested he listen for a while, start with small talk about the weather or a current event and gradually he would find his way.

And find his way he did. When he found the fellow guests were friendly, he became less self-conscious and as his comfort level rose, his natural wit was liberated. At times, he could not suppress it. Most times it showed up as a spontaneous response to something he heard, maybe a quick connection to another meaning. Once a friend of mine touted the skill of her chiropractor, constantly referring to him as her "chiro." Tom afterward innocently asked, "Isn't it rather expensive to go to Egypt for treatment?" Groan. Obviously, Tom enjoyed puns and he liked to indicate this was his form of "pun"ishment.

Once in the teacher's lounge a colleague who was a staunch believer in horoscopes was checking everyone's zodiac sign. She finally got to Tom and asked, "What sign are you under, Tom?" He replied, " I'm under the 'No Parking this side Tuesdays and Thursdays 9-11 AM' sign. "

Tom had favorite quips for special occasions. If he was friendly with the groom, he offered his congratulations after the wedding ceremony with this comment, "Now you'll know the true meaning of happiness" - pregnant pause - "and it will be too late!" Another one was for guests after saying their farewells at the end of a visit with us; we would stand at our door and wave a final good-bye. When they were almost out of ear shot, Tom would say loudly with clear relief in his voice, "At last, they're gone!"

Sometimes Tom's humor missed the mark, the comment unappreciated and better left unsaid. But, he always tried. In this case, Maria, a tennis teammate of mine, wanted to pay her luncheon fee that I was collecting. When she saw Tom, she asked if he would give me the money. Seeing her concern about the money reaching me, he couldn't resist. He said, "Well, I'm going to the races this afternoon; I might want to bet this money." Taken aback by this unexpected reply, she retracted her request very apologetically. Tom, so dismayed by her reaction, by her discomfort, quickly said he'd be glad to take the money to me. Too late. Maria showed she was not to be toyed with. She calmly thanked him, declined his offer, and went on her way. This was one time Tom did not leave his audience laughing. This audience left Tom almost crying.

Adding spice and fun to ordinary situations was a way of life for Tom. With appropriate, deliberate, creative details, he usually had satisfying results. My niece Patty at thirteen years old had a solo guitar performance for the end-of-year recital. She was excited about it and her enthusiasm fired up Tom's imagination about making it memorable. The evening after the program Tom called her and disguised his voice by sticking his tongue to one side of his mouth. During the conversation he stuttered severely, spoke slowly, and breathed heavily. He commented on her pretty looks and managed to say, "You play pretty good, too." Completely baffled by this call, Patty was speechless. She finally found her voice when Tom asked her for a date. She quickly blurted, "My mother doesn't let me go out with boys!"

Tom was delighted with this prank and he had to enjoy it with one more step. Some time later while talking to Patty, he made oblique references to the recital and dating until the light bulb went on. Patty then realized the anonymous nut on the phone was none other than her Uncle Tom. She was had.

There was another phone call remembered in the words of Kim, daughter of a good friend, Tom Hamilton.

"It was when I was ten years old and very sick in the hospital. I had been there longer than expected

and was starting to feel pretty low when I received a call from my truant officer who told me I was in big trouble for missing too much school. In a panic, I tried to explain, but to no avail. Then the details of my punishment for this truant behavior began to sound sillier and sillier until my truant officer revealed his identity as the clever Mr. Morgan. I laughed and laughed for the first time in weeks.

"You would think I'd learned my lesson, but it was not the last time he would fool me with a phone prank. He startled me a few years later when a caller announced in a heavy accent that he was 'Vladimir from the Russian Embassy' about some important business with my father. I got a good laugh then, too."

One evening we went to a Mets game at Shea Stadium in New York. Sitting in our bleacher seats behind first base, Tom did what vocal fans usually do - shout jeers at the visiting team and cheers for the home team. Tom was nothing if not an avid fan. A Hispanic couple sat in front of us and a young man with his teen-age brother sat next to Tom. After a couple of innings I saw the shoulders of the man in front shake with laughter after a few of Tom's taunts. The man next to Tom started laughing too and his brother leaned over to ask, "What did he say?" This reaction followed most of Tom's comments. During the seventh inning stretch the Hispanic fellow turned around, smiled timidly, and said a few words in Spanish to Tom who just smiled back and nodded. It seemed the fellow understood the baseball chatter in English, but was not fluent in the language. When the game ended, the Hispanic fan looked back at Tom and shook hands with him. The man used the human touch to indicate how much he enjoyed hearing the shouts of encouragement for the Mets and those of abuse for the visiting players. The seat mate next to Tom also acknowledged the baseball banter he heard and said that this was the most enjoyable baseball game he ever attended. This was vintage Tom. Wherever he was he had fun, had a good time and so did the people around him.

Tom's most creative and most successful caper was set in a small town bistro in central Jersey. The restaurant served good food and offered the usual entertainment: vocal and instrumental music, a belly dancer, and announcements to honor birthdays and anniversaries.

We suggested dinner there one night for four couples. This was a new venue for the other three couples and, yes, Tom wanted it to be special for our friends. He felt a bit apprehensive about recommending an eatery because certain elements were out of his control like food and service, but he could control the addition of fun. Tom went to work. When he made the reservations, he asked if they would recognize visiting dignitaries. The receptionist said they would be honored and delighted to do so and instructed Tom to write the specifics on a note to give the hostess when we arrived. None of the others was privy to this scenario. Tom just wanted to set the scene, cast the characters, watch the action, if any, and enjoy the results, hopefully.

On the appointed evening we reached the restaurant in good time and Tom unobtrusively handed the hostess his note which listed his guests as the mayor, council chairman, and police chief, all of Chelsea, New Hampshire, a fictitious place, naturally. After the waitress took our drink orders, the host/owner came to greet us warmly and asked how things were in New England. This puzzled our group, all from New Jersey and New York, but Tom knew his friends. Ed Tavss was never at a loss for words and he didn't disappoint us this time. He thought this question was a bit odd, but the fellow was friendly, so he would be friendly, too. Ed replied with general comments about the area available to any reader of the news. Next the host asked specifically who was minding the store back home? Not to be outdone, Ed was now eager to engage in dialogue and again gave sensible answers. When the host left, Roberta, Ed's wife, said, "How nice. They're so friendly here." I elbowed Tom, barely able to contain myself. Act One went over very well.

Midway through the entertainment, the host stepped into the

spotlight and announced celebratory days for some diners. Then, he said. "Tonight we are honored to have special guests from New England." Ed looked up alertly, so that's the New England connection, and peered around to see these New Englanders. The host continued, "Please give a warm welcome to the mayor of Chelsea, New Hampshire." The spotlight swung around the room and stopped at our table searching for a person to focus on. Tom delightedly directed his little show and motioned a surprised Ed to rise and acknowledge the growing applause. As the light settled on Ed, the bewildered look slowly left his face and he finally gathered what was going on. It was delicious, exquisite to see the understanding spread across his face. He was roped in, on the spot, in the spotlight. He had little choice but to play out the part. And like the trouper we expected, he did. With a knowing glance and a nod to Tom, he rose slowly, seemingly shy as befitting a small town politician in a big city, and gave a slight wave of his hand. By this time, Roberta wanted to slide under the table. Little did the audience know that the "mayor" was a scientist with a major chemical firm. The host named more "officials" - city council chairman who was Bob our neighbor in New Jersey and police chief Jim who was a retiree from the New York City police force. Tom happily pointed the spotlight to our other friends who slowly stood and graciously acknowledged the same warm applause. When our group settled down after receiving the acclaim attached to the celebrity status of politicians, Tom and I applauded our friends who cooperated and, by now, not too reluctantly got into the "act." They made Tom's scenario wildly successful, going beyond all expectations. Act Two was a smash hit.

After the applause subsided, the "actors" realized the audience thought they really were from New England. They did act! They started congratulating themselves, enjoying their foray into improvisation. At this time our waitress interrupted our self-praise for their "acting" and Tom's role as creative director by opening a magnum of champagne, compliments of the host. We had to keep Roberta from hiding under the table. She didn't want to have any part of this scene.

As we left the bistro, folks came over to offer their own personal greetings. Ed, now having fun as "mayor," threw himself into the role and made the appropriate responses, reveling in the attention. The host thanked us for coming and, when Ed invited him to visit in Chelsea, we literally pulled at his coat sleeves to get him away from the well-wishers and bade our farewells before the bubble burst. Act Three - the perfect ending.

In the parking lot, we could hardly contain ourselves, aching from laughter. This story had and continues to have a long life. We four couples have retold and relived it often, enjoying it each time. Tom gave us a memory filled with laughs for a lifetime. Here's to the mayor of Chelsea, New Hampshire, courtesy of Tom Morgan.

We never returned to this restaurant. To disclose our true identity would spoil this story.

Humor can arise from the most unexpected sources. Tom always railed vehemently against false advertising. While watching a television commercial, he would shout, "Do they think we are stupid enough to believe that?" Another condition he found irksome was the free advertising on clothing. He removed all logos he could. He would have taken off the company insignias on our cars if he could have filled in the holes that remained.

Ah, but with Tom Morgan creativity he found satisfaction against this kind of commercialism by using the ubiquitous baseball cap. He had the words "My Hat" ironed onto his baseball caps. No more "Budweiser" or "John Deere" caps for Tom. This phrase hit a responsive chord among the passers-by. Many of them smiled at Tom in recognition of and agreement with his reason for his personal logo on his cap. Most men had to engage in repartee.

"So, that's 'My Hat'," from the oncoming stroller.

"No, this is not your hat," was Tom's immediate reply.

"But it says 'My Hat'."

"I know, but it's not your hat." Smiles from everybody who saw and heard this exchange.

Another opening comment was, "So, that's your hat."

Tom's comeback was, "No, it's my hat."

"That's what I said, your hat."

Tom had the last words, "No, it's not your hat; it's my hat."

This banter continued whenever we passed onlookers who felt compelled to address the notation on Tom's cap. Others too shy to speak up, nudged their companions to take a look at Tom's cap.

The most original remark came from a female airline attendant who greeted passengers entering the plane. Seeing Tom's cap, she quickly quipped,

"So that's where my hat is."

That was a rare time when Tom was caught speechless, but only momentarily. He smiled and told her he found it at a garage sale.

Tom in "My Hat" with Ruth

The "My Hat" cap had such an unexpected popular response whenever Tom wore it, he decided to expand his cap wardrobe. They included "Down One" for bridge, "Gizadeech" and "Say Wha?" for people from the Bronx, and "RCB" for the Richey Concert Band in which he played second clarinet.

None of these later notations had the widespread, humorous reactions that "My Hat" had. That one generated a great deal of fun for all - for Tom, me, and the onlookers who noticed the cap. "My Hat" was a minor attempt by one man to retaliate against unpaid advertising, but it surprisingly reaped major rewards for many in humor. This was typical of Tom. He had a unique way to have fun, planned or unplanned.

The humor from "My Hat" was most serendipitous.

An ironic touch developed with "My Hat." After several years of performing in a band, very few members in the group knew his name. They referred to him as Mr. "My Hat." That was his identity.

In keeping with apparel, Tom bought a T-shirt with the statement on its front that read, "I'm walking with stupid here!" It ended with a hand pointing left. Whenever he wore it with me, I made sure he was on my left. That summer he wore it at the annual end-of-year picnic for teachers. Knowing people did not read the usually innocuous print on these shirts, he glad-handed everyone, placing all on his left. Eventually people caught on. However, before the administrators did, he warmly greeted them on his left side, and gleefully, audaciously posed for the shutterbugs, much to the delight of the staff.

A situation or a personal characteristic can also lead to amusement. The person with a sense of humor seizes any opportunity and creates a setting for others to enjoy.

Bob and Marge, our neighbors in central Jersey, were good friends, the kind you always want next door. Although they had regular jobs, Bob and Tom had the usual summer task of tending their own vegetable garden. After all, New Jersey is known as the Garden State if you ignore the New Jersey Turnpike, aka Cancer Alley. Bob and Tom chose different vegetables to grow but each raised the state's perennial favorite - the tomato, the famous, delicious Jersey tomato.

They were both easy going fellows with no psychological baggage- affable, congenial, non-competitive. However, Marge was a bit more competitive. Since she could see our garden from her kitchen window, she was eager to learn who would have the first ready-to-eat-tomato of the season. One year Tom decided to play with that. He burrowed among the boxes of Christmas decorations, found a red Christmas ball, and tied it to the highest branch of his tallest tomato bush. It was early July weeks before any tomato would ripen in New Jersey when he called to Marge who was at her kitchen window and pointed to the red ball. She smiled and said politely, feebly, "How nice." Naturally, she told her husband that Tom already had ripe tomatoes. Later that evening Bob came over and asked Tom how his tomatoes ripened so early.

Tom's reply, "Easy if you have red Christmas balls. They perform on demand." Marge forgave Tom because she liked him.

Sometimes the humor comes at the expense of another.

We befriended a young teacher named Jane while her husband, an ensign in the U.S. Navy, was serving a tour of duty on a destroyer. Both had just graduated from Ohio State University and had never been to the "Big Apple." When Robin, her husband, had his first leave, we invited them to our home for cocktails before going to dinner. During the preprandial pleasantries Tom saw a flicker of anxiety in Robin's eyes when he learned that we planned dinner at our favorite restaurant in Manhattan's Chinatown. That one little squint was just the opening Tom needed. Calmly he listed the delicacies we might try: 100 year old duck eggs, bird's nest soup made from a real bird's nest (a very expensive dish, by the way), pigeon, pigs' feet in whiskey with peanuts, but the best would be chicken feet soup- mmh, delicious. With each enumeration Robin's smile grew weaker, his color grew paler. But he was game, polite, and never said a word neither in praise nor in protest.

The tradition in Manhattan Chinatown restaurants was to reward their regular diners with the house soup as the first course, gratis. They made a big batch of soup to feed the waiters and there was always some for their favorite customers. This soup wasn't gourmet fare, but tasty home cooking. As we entered the Pell Street restaurant, the head waiter greeted us warmly, seated us, and asked if we wanted the house soup. We never refused that offer and assured Jane and Robin that they were in for a treat. The waiter placed the soup tureen in the middle of the table, lifted the lid, and, behold! chicken feet jutted from the soup at several different angles.

Robin's eyebrows almost reached his hairline and he would not go near that bowl of soup even if he had ten foot long chopsticks. Jane was more adventurous and drank the broth which was nothing more than a well-seasoned chicken soup. Tom could not have scripted a better scene.

The rest of the dinner selections proved not as exotic as Tom predicted. Most importantly, Jane and Robin enjoyed the rest of the dining experience.

Using different elements of humor, Tom amused many people. Their laughter as a result of something he said or did delighted him. The combination of his wit and humor made Tom an entertaining person. Of course, folks enjoyed themselves with him.

Part Seven
IRS Auditee

A few years into our marriage our combined earnings put us in the top tax bracket, but we were at the bottom of that bracket. That irked Tom. He thought there had to be a legitimate way to reduce our taxable income. After doing some research, he found the strategy of investing in rental property that allowed all expenses as tax deductions. The other component he added was out-of-state locations that could be desirable retirement areas. Tom was always thinking ahead, thinking down the road of life, way down the road.

Tom checked this idea with IRS agents in three different venues: one in Jersey City, another in Newark, and the third on the 800 number to assist tax payers. Strangely enough, they concurred that every expense was deductible for owners of rental property. However, all expenses had to be accurately documented with verification. That was no problem for two experienced teachers whose very existence depended on careful recordkeeping in their daily work.

Armed with this threefold corroboration, Tom eagerly and I reluctantly looked for possible rental homes in Florida, Tom's choice, and North Carolina, my choice. Two summers later we owned a small home in Florida and one in South Carolina. Tom filed our income taxes and filled out the proper schedules for these two out-of-state properties. The strategy worked; it reduced our taxable figure considerably.

When we received our third or fourth tax rebate, the IRS wanted to see firsthand what we did to achieve this distinction. The IRS called us in for an audit on the Florida home as filed in the tax form for a recent year. That notice unsettled me, but challenged Tom - typical female/male reactions. I was Venus; Tom was Mars.

He said, "Everything is legal according to three IRS agents. We went by the book. Not to worry." Easy for him to say; difficult for me to feel calm about an audit.

Tom took a day off from school for this IRS appointment. He went dressed as usual for a work day - white shirt, tie, sport jacket, and slacks. But, instead of carrying his attache case filled with students' homework papers, his rollbook and planbook, he lugged a carton about the size of a milk crate crammed with papers, records, receipts, everything that was related to the Florida home.

Although the appointment was scheduled for mid-morning, it was close to noon when the agent called Tom for his interview. Quick to note current conditions, opportunistic Tom plunked the heavy carton of records onto the agent's desk. Ever the chess player, Tom established his opening gambit. Noting the time, he calmly said it would be all right with him if the agent wanted to take an early lunch since this meeting might take a while and Tom was free all day anyway, no need for him to get back to school. Can you imagine the agent's reaction? Here was an auditee concerned with the auditor having his proper lunch time and poised for a long session?

"Oh, no, Mr. Morgan, it's all right. We can proceed."

"Fine," replied Tom, but he wasn't finished. "Before we start, I want you to note my occupation on my income tax form is listed as educator. You might like to know that I'm an English teacher and most of us want to write. I've always wanted to write a play about the IRS. I'm looking forward to this meeting. It should give me lots of material to use." I don't think this agent was ready for Tom.

With that introduction over, they got down to business. Paper after paper, document after document, receipt after receipt passed between them. Not only did Tom have an itemization of expenses but he had a narrative to supplement it. From the jam packed box he could not find the narrative for one of the two trips to Florida that year. The agent must have been glad to find that flaw in Tom's presentation and scheduled another meeting for Tom to bring the missing narrative to complete the audit. Tom did not like the idea of taking another day from school and suggested his wife bring it in that day. The agent agreed and Tom went home satisfied. He believed the agent could not find any item to be denied as a deduction for this property.

Two weeks later it was my turn to face the IRS representative. Encouraged by Tom's confidence, I was not intimidated. Actually, the agent unwittingly erased any apprehensions I might have had. The first question he asked me was, "Would you take 75% of the rebate?" He had asked Tom if he would take 50% of the rebate. Naturally, Tom refused. Now the agent was offering a bigger amount to us.

That angered me and, indignantly I blurted out, "Why would I accept that? We want 100% of the rebate! All the money we spent is legitimate. This is a legal rental property as confirmed by a few IRS agents we consulted in different locations in New Jersey. And, I didn't want to invest this way. Tom had to talk me into this. I don't even like Florida!"

Obviously, my answer to his question was an emphatic, "No!"

That was when I gave him the missing narrative Tom did not submit during the last session. I mentioned it was in the carton, but Tom just overlooked it. The agent wasn't listening, he was reading Tom's report. After a couple of minutes I heard him mutter to himself, "This guy is something else."

Hearing that, I was sure we were home free. When the agent completed reading that narrative, he returned it to me and ended the meeting by saying, "You should receive our decision in several weeks."

With Tom's solicitous, disarming, bold comments and my righteous indignation, and with all the necessary proof, the IRS had to conclude that not only did we tell the truth but that we also deserved and earned the entire amount of that year's rebate.

Several weeks later the IRS sent us a form indicating that the audit was completed and our return for that year was accepted as submitted!

Hooray for Tom, one of the unusual guys who eagerly awaited an audit by the IRS.

Tom never did write that play about the IRS, although others did. William Zandt and Jane Milmore co-wrote "Love, Sex, and the IRS" in 1980.

Part Eight

Belated Genealogist

Tom, always interested in his Irish heritage, bemoaned that he had only sketchy information on the background of his mother.

Margaret Reilly, Tom's mother, led a Cinderella's life. Her parents were Jerome O'Reilly of County Cork and Nora Mullins O'Reilly of County Mayo, Irish immigrants in New York. Jerome became a reporter for the old <u>New York World</u>, a Manhattan daily newspaper, and her mother, who became a charwoman in the home of a local judge, died in the flu epidemic of 1917-18. Widower Jerome and Margaret, who was three years old, went to live in a rooming house owned by an Irish widow, a Mrs. McCarthy with two young daughters. Unfortunately, Jerome survived his wife by only a few years. When he was 48 years old, word came to the rooming house that he had died. Margaret never learned the circumstances of her father's death.

Now orphaned , Margaret was alone in the world at the age of eight. The owner of the boarding house took in Margaret and reared her. Her motivations were probably not only altruistic but also pragmatic. The "old lady," as she was called, could not throw this little girl out on the streets after the O'Reillys now Reillys had lived in the house for some years. That heartless action would surely draw protests from the other boarders. Besides, Margaret would be a companion for her two girls and, most importantly, she would be another free hand to help with the many chores related to running her hostelry. She became an Irish Cinderella in this household.

One story from her childhood that Mom told Tom took place when she was about twelve. One boarder always asked one of the girls to get him a "tin" of beer at the local saloon just up the street, a common errand for youngsters then. He would tip the daughters as gofers but not the orphan. One day Mom was tired of being left out of the money. She kept one coin from the change after she made the purchase. Knowing the skinflint would ask about the shorted change, she put the coin in her mouth. As expected, he asked for the missing coin when she returned. She just shook her head in ignorance. Infuriated, he demanded to see her hands. Happily she opened them - empty! Beside himself, he suddenly thrust his face close to hers and shouted menacing words. Margaret was so scared she gulped, swallowing the coin, and scrambled away from the madman. The miser did not get his coin but neither did Margaret get the pleasure of spending that purloined coin as she wished. Was there a lesson in this incident for the young girl? Crime does not pay?

The realization that his mother had no memories of her father and mother haunted Tom. As an adult he tried to fill this void. Armed with only their names and approximate dates of death, he tried to locate the graves of his maternal grandparents Reilly in New York. No success. Trying to find something, anything about them, he spent many hours at the National Archives, Bayonne Military Ocean Terminal in New Jersey, poring over passenger lists of ships leaving Ireland and England about the time they might have immigrated to the United States. This was another futile attempt.

Now with Tom Morgan, Tom's father, that was another story. Tom, the senior, was one of six children who were born and raised in County Roscommon, Ireland. As the youngest of three sons, he had no prospects of owning land. Since the older brothers left the homestead to make their way in the world, that left Tom home to work the farm for and with his parents. At this time the British conscripted all available males in Ireland. To escape the army, he and a friend slipped away to England without a word to any one. He found work as a jack-of-all-trades and found a girl to marry. Sadly, his young wife died suddenly. Because his elder sisters were immigrants in the United States, he decided to try his luck in the New World, too. There was no going back to Ireland.

Tom Morgan of Roscommon, Ireland, landed in New York, and, as fate would have it, he rented a room in the boarding house where Margaret Reilly lived and worked. A few years later Prince Charming Morgan and Cinderella Reilly married and had two children, a second generation of a Margaret and a Tom.

From the time Dad Morgan left Ireland, he never contacted his family. All news from the old homestead reached him through his sisters in Chicago. Understandably, Tom, junior, had little knowledge of his parents' forebears, but he knew the counties and villages in Ireland that the Reillys and Morgans called home.

Over the years Tom, junior, had given much thought to his Ireland connection. That thought transformed into action when he received a letter from his second cousin Sandra Doherty of Chicago. She had an assignment from her high school English teacher to develop her family tree and asked Tom for help. In giving Sandra the names of the descendants of the Morgans in the United States, Tom realized the family tree would not include ancestors and their children still in Ireland. This realization spurred his determination to contact any living relatives there, to open lines of communication with them after decades of silence, to learn of his ancestors, to have a genealogical history, finally.

Eagerly we planned Tom's first visit to Ireland, not only to see the sights, but also to fulfill the dream of finding kin. Our trip started with a flight to Shannon Airport where we rented a car and toured the country using the ubiquitous Bed and Breakfast Inns. We had no reservations just listings and ratings for these operations and managed quite well. Following the popular route along the southwest coast, we unsurprisingly enjoyed the gentle, scenic slopes of verdant countryside and surprisingly savored the excellent food. Nothing better tasting than fresh fish served simply with little enhancement beyond its own natural flavor.

With the town of Skibbereen behind us, we got on the track to trace the ancestors of Tom's mother in County Cork. The route led to the villages of Knockatlewig (pronounced nock-a-to-wee), Rossmore, and Castle Ventre. We marveled at the handwritten, gracefully scripted, legible names of baptized children in church records over 100 years old. No pot of gold at the end of this trail.

Tom had better luck in County Down. Tom's godfather, John McElherron, had retired to Warrenpoint. Not only was this town on the eastern shore of the country, but it was in the northern part of Ireland governed by the British. Regardless of the political problems, Tom was determined to go. He could not, would not miss this opportunity. It was John who took the young Tom fishing, hunting, and swimming and gave him wonderful childhood memories. When John, a guard at a Manhattan art museum, married Bena, an employee of Fanny Farmer's, they decided to spend the twilight of their years in Warrenpoint, County Down, Ireland. Although Tom's visit was to their grave sites, it was heartwarming for him to put flowers on their graves and pray for their souls in St. Peter's Church, which John and Bena attended. Tom found a connection of kinship in the old country, at long, long last.

With this first memorable milestone in his pursuit for kinfolk behind him, we headed to northwestern Ireland. Again the ride was highlighted by the glories of the Irish countryside. After enjoying picture postcard scenery and visiting some major sites in this territory, we reached Donegal and turned southeastward on the road to County Roscommon and the town of Ballintubber to find the Morgan connection.

We stopped for gas in Ballinlough about five miles from our destination. Tom asked the service attendant if he knew of any Morgans in Ballintubber. I looked sideways at Tom with raised eyebrows, silently signifying, "You've got to be kidding! What would he know about residents in a town five miles down the road?" The attendant said he heard of two Morgan families there and we could get more information at the railroad station in Castlerea, the town next to Ballintubber. Tom looked sideways at me with raised eyebrows, silently signifying, "So, what do you know, smartie!" If the proverbial feather were around, it would have knocked me off my feet.

At the Castlerea railroad station we made our inquiry and learned of a Morgan who was a green grocer selling produce from a red van. Wonderful combination of colors. No red van was there, but an old man nearby identified a car owned by a Morgan. Tom left a note about our quest on the windshield of that car. We took a room at the local hotel, had dinner, and walked around the town. Tom saw an attendant at the hotel's car park and asked if he knew of Morgans in Ballintubber. I received my second shock in gathering information about people in rural Ireland - everybody knows everybody regardless of distance.

His answer, "Yes, there is a grieving widow Morgan who's also lost her son. Follow that road to Ballintubber."

We had to follow that lead. The next morning driving along that country road to Ballintubber, we saw a few teen-age girls walking by the roadside. Tom stopped and said, "My name is Morgan and we're from the United States. We're looking for Morgans in this area."

One teen-ager replied, "Well, I'm a Morgan. Speak to my Mam in the house behind you."

Immediately we made a U-turn. Tom went to the door; I stayed in the car in case this was another dead-end. A woman opened the door, and Tom repeated,

"My name is Morgan and I'm from the States looking for Morgans in Ballintubber."

The woman smiled, opened her arms, drew Tom inside, saying, in a delightful brogue, rolling her r's and prolonging her l's,

"Well, if you're a Morgan, you're welcome here."

I was close enough to hear her warm, sincere greeting, and my eyes welled up with tears that spilled over. It seemed Tom had reached journey's end, a homecoming his father never made, never even dreamed of. He was in the home of Kathleen Morgan, widow of Gerald Morgan, Tom's first cousin.

The young girl who directed us to her home was Eithne Morgan, Tom's second cousin, youngest of the five daughters of Kathleen and Gerald Morgan.

A bonus was a visitor in Kathleen's home at that time, a Sally Towey. She actually knew Tom's father and told us that young Tom of Ballintubber was the best looking man in town. He taught her sister to dance. We learned that he also was a singer and melodeon player, an all-round character, today's swinger. Where did he find the time to develop these skills and talents while doing all the farm work? Well, the winter nights on a farm can be long.

Kathleen Morgan, left, and Sally Towey

Kathleen Morgan's daughters (L to R) Mary, Patricia, Eithne, Sheila

We met Kathleen's good-looking daughters, all five of them, and one son-in-law. Before going up the road a short piece to meet Martin Morgan, the oldest of Tom's cousins, we arranged for the clan to gather after church at Garvey's, the only pub in town, the pub where Tom's father had beers as a young man.

That was very special for Tom. Kathleen demurred, having done nothing socially since the tragic death of her husband. Encouraging her to join us, Tom said,

"There comes a time when - - - - - ," and he trailed off.

"Yes," she responded, "there comes a time."

Then I added, "We've come a long way."

"Yes," Kathleen murmured, "you've come a long way."

This was typical dialogue in Ireland: subdued, understated, repetitious, silences fraught with meanings which were readily understood.

The upshot - Kathleen came to Garvey's after church that Saturday. Her daughters were thrilled. One of them said,

"In five years she hasn't done anything. It's about time."

Kathleen left earlier than the others. But, come she did.

Tom, Martin and Marie Morgan with daughter Breda

Tom went to Ireland in a search for his blood connection. Finding this bonanza of relatives went beyond his expectations. He discovered one first cousin and his wife, the widow of another first cousin, and twenty nine second cousins. Meeting all of them was one of the most emotional and satisfying experiences of his life. A fulfillment of a dream he held for decades.

Other memorable events took place in Ballintubber. After hearing the many stories and activities of his father's young life in the "old country," Tom thoroughly enjoyed cavorting among the ruins of the castle where his father played, standing on the spot where his father was born, looking over the fields where his father farmed, drinking beer in the same pub where his father drank his pints. Truly, a homecoming tapestry woven through a lifetime of threads from tales told by father to son.

Martin, left, and Tom on original Morgan homesite now owned by Kathleen Morgan

Tom on the ruins of Ballintubber Castle

Part Nine

Accomplished Amateur

Now facing retirement, Tom did not plan to fade into the sunset. During his study of English literature at Seton Hall University, he discovered some of his own philosophy expressed precisely in Alfred Tennyson's "Ulysses."

"Old age hath yet his honor and his toil.
Death closes all; but something ere this end,
Some work of noble note, may yet be done,
Not unbecoming men who strove with the Gods."

Tom's work of noble note for his "old age" was rooted in his teens. In high school one of Tom's friends joined the school band and played the clarinet. This was the first time Tom heard that instrument and found the sound very pleasant. In a few years he concluded that playing the clarinet would be placed on his "to-do" list for the future.

As a young adult Tom listened to the New York City radio station WNEW, particularly to the "Make Believe Ballroom" with deejays Martin Block and William B. Williams. Listening to this popular music provided a soothing background that helped him get through the late evening hours of study while getting his college degree at night. Over time that kind of music with jazz interpretations became his listening favorite.

When we started dating, Tom and I discovered a mutual interest in this music, and on one of our first dates we went to the Red Blazer in Greenwich Village. It had sawdust on the floor, ten cent hot dogs boiled in beer, but the real attraction for Tom was "our kind" of music performed live. That evening we heard a clarinetist, a guitarist, and a drummer. Later, Gene Krupa sat in for a set. What a bonus! The music was very good, and the clarinetist was outstanding. We learned his name was Kenny Davern and we tried to find where he had other gigs for us to attend and continue hearing his marvelous sound. We were unsuccessful.

In the mid-seventies we became suburbanites by moving to central Jersey. Our neighbors who knew of our particular musical interest told us of a new restaurant nearby with live music. Our thinking was "no harm in trying." We struck gold! Entering the Cornerstone in Metuchen, New Jersey, we found an intimate atmosphere, good food, convivial patrons, friendly staff, congenial owner, and good music with an excellent clarinetist. The owner/ host, an affable fellow and good restaurateur, stopped by all the tables to greet his customers. When he reached us, we gave him positive comments about the restaurant, but Tom really wanted the name of the clarinetist. The host's reply was, "Oh, that's Kenny Davern." Serendipity! After a decade of hearing nothing from Davern we found him, many miles removed from Manhattan, appearing regularly almost at our doorstep. Musical paradise! We spoke to Kenny at the break and never lost touch with him since.

Because John Swain, the owner/host of the Cornerstone loved this kind of music and paid well for this love, many good musicians played here. With this reputation, others players who finished gigs early would come here and jam with the paid performers. Metuchen, a bedroom community of Manhattan, was easily accessible to the metropolitan area drawing many quality musicians. Often the best music at the Cornerstone came during these late hour jam sessions. This bistro became a favorite source of musical entertainment and drew us there regularly. It was popular with quite a few other fans from all over the state and nearby towns in Pennsylvania. The place became our special jazz club.

After hearing Davern again, Tom remembered his boyhood dream of playing the clarinet. He renewed that pledge, determined to make it a reality. A few years before his retirement he bought a used clarinet at a pawnshop in Newark, New Jersey. He had never held this instrument before. Now, the moment of truth. Would he be able to play it? Fidgeting with a new mouthpiece and new reeds, positioning the instrument in his mouth, he tried. He huffed and he puffed, and he almost blew himself up. He became flushed with the exertion and looked apoplectic. However, as I expected, Tom persisted, made the necessary adjustments, and in a couple of days coaxed a sound from the instrument.

Determined to learn to play, he engaged an elementary school instrumental music teacher, Tom Bardar, and practiced diligently, daily. How diligently you may ask? We traveled frequently often taking three to four week trips. The first thing I packed was my make-up. The first items Tom packed were his clarinet and a three ring book filled with his favorite songs in all keys. That was his travel music book. He kept to a daily schedule of playing wherever we traveled. I wonder what he would have done if he were a drummer or a bass violist? The highlight of one jazz cruise came at the end of one practice session in our cabin. Answering a knock on the door, Tom expected to hear a request for no more music. Imagine his reaction when the person who knocked identified himself as the occupant of the next cabin and wanted to tell Tom how much they all enjoyed his music. What a high for Tom! The wannabe actually became what he wanted to be.

After settling in our retirement home in Port Richey with no contacts, we reached out to find activities we enjoyed: for both of us playing bridge and tennis, and for Tom playing his clarinet. In fact, Tom's musical aim was to find other old folks, instrumentalists like him, form a trio or quartet, and amuse the older folks residing in assisted living facilities which exist in abundance in Florida. That was Tom's noble effort during his years of leisure.

One of our new bridge-playing friends, an accomplished pianist, organist, keyboardist herself, suggested that Tom contact Henry Fletcher, director of the Richey Concert Band, to see if Tom could fit in with that group. Although Tom had been playing only four years, he had no second thoughts about that suggestion. In early 1994 we attended a performance by this concert band which had three clarinetists and about forty five other players on reeds and horns. An amateur group that produced a great sound, it had a wonderful mix of musicians: young, old, men, women, retired professionals, competent amateurs, elementary school, high school, college students, and music teachers. Imagine, the clarinetist playing in the first seat was a dentist with a thriving practice. Not knowing what to expect, Tom approached the director at the end of the concert and broached the subject of joining the group. Mr. Fletcher, an amiable fellow, welcomed Tom warmly and said, "If you can read music, you can join us now. Practice is Tuesday nights." As simply as that Tom became a member of the Richey Concert Band.

Ignorance is bliss. At that first practice session Tom received the third part clarinet sheet music for the sixteen pieces to be played at the next concert about a month off. Tom had so much to learn. Performing in this band was so different from playing solo for his music teacher. Here he had to join three other musicians who were reading the music for the first and second clarinet parts while he was reading the music for the third part. And, he was the only one playing third at this time. He had no person playing the same part to ask for help. He was entirely on his own. Tom had difficulty in learning when to stop playing and when to resume playing. Following the arrangement for the piece, the entire clarinet section, first, second, and third parts had their separate music to play the melody or harmony. In the meantime,

The Richey Concert Band directed by Henry Fletcher at the end of a performance with Tom in the first row, second from left

following the same arrangement the rest of the band - other reeds, woodwinds, brass, and percussion did exactly the same as the clarinet section- played their own parts for the music. One begins to appreciate the arranger for his talent, ear, and musicality. In one piece he or she writes the melody for the first clarinet, the harmony for the second clarinet, the lower harmony for the third clarinet. And repeats this for the other instruments in the band.

Tom had to put in several hours of practice daily to keep up with the other clarinetists. Performing in concerts after playing the clarinet only four or five years proved difficult. It was exquisitely rewarding but supremely daunting. With two of these musicales behind him, Tom thought he would not return to the band for the next season, thinking he could not keep up with the other performers. I observed he was getting better and had to give himself more than three months with the band to make the transition from

Warming up for an outdoor concert

a solo amateur performer/learner to an integral member of a band with seventy or eighty instrumentalists, all of them with better training and more experience. This new venture also involved a cross-over from popular music to Sousa marches in fast time and light classical pieces interspersed with main-stream standards, all to large audiences some numbering around a thousand. He remained unconvinced. However, at the last concert of the season in May before the summer break, when the director was bidding his farewells to the members, he saw Tom, and quickly, firmly, intuitively said, "I'll see you here next September." With this vote of confidence, this simple statement of expectation from the pro, the director, Tom committed himself to this band.

The first few years Tom practiced many hours daily to prepare for the concerts. By the third year, the daily number of playing hours decreased to just a few. After reaching this level of competence, he bought a clarinet from Le Blanc, the company that manufactured Pete Fontaine's clarinets. Feeling confident about his clarinet playing, he had to get to the next level which was to expand his musical capability. That led to the purchase of an alto saxophone and the necessary lessons.

So proficient did Tom become with both these instruments he was asked to play them in two other bands - the Strings and Strutters and the Deutchmeister Blas Band. The latter had its members clothed in lederhosen and Alpine hats. Once when he was wearing this outfit, a ninety year old woman told him he had nice legs! Tom reached another milestone in his old age when he received a check from the Deutchmeister band for several performances during October Fest season. He exclaimed, "I'm a paid musician now!" His original plan was to play music with two or three other amateurs to small audiences of older folks. He became second clarinet in a section of ten or more clarinetists in a band with upwards of eighty members to audiences that often neared a thousand. He was playing two instruments in three bands. No longer a wannabe, Tom was truly a musician, a performer. He was euphoric.

*Tom in full gear as Deutchmeister band
member with his alto sax*

Tom's new musical ventures included one solo performance. During our early years in Port Richey Tom played chess at a Senior Center in the next town of Hudson and met Jack Ennis who became quite attached to Tom and treated him like the son he didn't have. A few years later Jack's wife Betty passed away after a brief illness. While discussing funeral arrangements with Tom, Jack was upset because the church organist was not available for the service. How sad he thought that there would be no music for his wife. Without hesitation Tom offered to fill in with his clarinet. On the day of Betty's funeral prayers were interspersed by clear, soft strains of "Amazing Grace" and "Nearer My God to Thee" that flowed from Tom's instrument and wafted through the church. Hearing that music, I felt tears of sympathy and pride meander down my cheeks and I let them dry there. And, as often happens, Jack followed his beloved in a few months and his children asked Tom to play for him.

This was a venue that Tom never dreamed for a performance, but he was profoundly gratified to give this loving, musical tribute to his friends, Jack and Betty Ennis.

Playing the clarinet in retirement for the enjoyment of audiences in his local area, Tom accomplished his final goal. This was his work of noble note, something to be done before the end.

Part Ten

Responsible Godfather

A different personal relationship developed for Tom at the beginning of his retirement. When my nephew Kivin Chin and his wife Dorothy had a baby boy, they chose Tom to be their boy's godfather. In a subsequent conversation with Kivin, Tom learned why he was selected for this role. Kivin not only loved and respected his uncle-in-law, but also liked Tom's philosophy of life, his zest for living, his desire to explore many activities, his sense of fun in all his endeavors. Thus, he hoped that Nicholas would absorb some of these traits from being closely involved with Tom. Hearing these reasons explained to him, Tom was honored to be Nicholas's godfather.

When Nicholas turned five years old, his father passed away. With this turn of events, Tom felt the full weight of his responsibility to be a godfather. We moved from New Jersey to Florida the year after Kivin's early demise. Even with that long distance separating us, we saw Nicholas frequently. Every year since Nicholas was five, he and his mother visited us in Florida during the Easter holidays.

Keeping Nicholas busy while he visited us was Tom's main objective. Nicholas returned the favor. At this time he was a bundle of energy. He did not know the word "walk;" he only knew the word "run." He was the embodiment of the word "run." Tom tried to keep up with the boy who found a new playmate. Nicholas followed Tom everywhere even into the bathroom where the line was drawn and a lesson was taught on closed doors. Once after some non-stop action, Nicholas asked Tom who was resting,

"What do we do next, Uncle Tom?"

"We do naps," Tom answered.

"What's that?" from the boy.

"I'll show you; follow me," Tom said. With that he led

Nicholas to the master bedroom, climbed onto the bed, put his head on the pillow, and said, "I'm sleeping for half an hour. That's a nap. Close the door on your way out and wake me later."

"Oh, okay, Uncle Tom," said a disappointed boy.

Role reversal, the adult required a rest from the activities with a perpetual motion youngster.

What did Tom teach Nicholas at Easter times? The boy learned to bait a hook, set the hook in the mouth of the fish, and reel in the fish on a small rod. He first fished from our dock and, after gaining skill with these techniques, he fished from our boat in the canal and the river. When he was old enough, Nicholas fished from a headboat in the Gulf of Mexico with veteran fishermen. Playing chess and shooting pool were new activities for him. Already with some experience as a swimmer and cyclist, Nicholas swam in the local community pool and in our canal and wheeled a bike around the neighborhood. He even rode to the shopping mall a few miles north. The latter trip was taken with another bicyclist, his mother. Of course, there were the obligatory trips to Tampa's Busch Gardens for the different rides and exhibits.

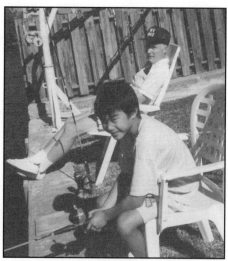

Tom with Nicholas fishing
in canal behind our home

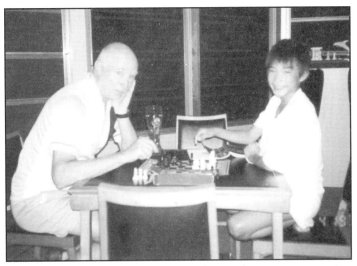

Tom and Nicholas playing chess

It was nothing but fun and games for Nicholas. One year Tom hid two dozen plastic Easter colored eggs in the house, in the garden, and in the boat. Nicholas knew the number of hidden eggs and the challenge was to gather all of them in a set time. His total found was 90 percent. Another time Tom planned a naval treasure hunt with clues. Using a map, Nicholas reached the first clue which led to the next, four in all. The clues were hidden in places that could only be reached by boat. They were scattered along the canal, on the bank of the river, and in a small cove across the river. Rowing the LOO'T II, Nicholas completed the hunt which took two days. The treasure was $25 in a water proof container. Of course, Tom accompanied the rower on every leg of the search.

All wasn't play in Florida, but Nicholas knew it would be fun just to be with Uncle Tom and do anything with him. Both looked forward to these annual Spring weeks knowing they thoroughly enjoyed being with each other. Occasionally, Tom would ask Nicholas to help him with some small chores like hosing the long, wide driveway, washing the car, digging some holes for plants. To insure Nicholas would agree, he added the incentive of some money if he finished the task satisfactorily. In this manner, Nicholas knew he had to follow instructions, complete the job, and do his best to reap the reward. For a ten to twenty minute stint of work, he received five to ten dollars. Not a bad wage for a ten year old. As night follows day, Tom emphasized the advantages of saving. If money is earned, a small portion should be put away in a safe place for future use. Since Nicholas had a bank account in his elementary school, this recommendation was a reinforcement of a practice by the school. Tom strongly urged that Nicholas save some of his money by putting it into this school account.

Not only was Tom instilling the value of a work ethic in Nicholas, but he was also giving him the pleasure of receiving some money as a reward for something, even if not for work. Part of this instruction was buried in Tom's past. While a youth in the Bronx, Tom's mother had a best friend, Betty Mansell. Tom considered her just one short step below his mother. Whenever they had a visit with Betty, there was a farewell ritual for Tom. She gave him a warm hug and put a quarter in his hand for being a good boy. He always looked forward to receiving that 25 cent piece and he remembered that gift fondly through the years. That same pleasant feeling Tom hoped to pass on to Nicholas.

Athletic attempts like catching ball, batting a ball, playing tennis did not attract Nicholas. He did play the clarinet for a few years, but that was a passing fancy. There was no guarantee that everything Tom tried hoping to arouse some long-lasting interest would be successful. No matter what the result, he believed he had to make the effort. One topic always explored for Nicholas's benefit was his father. Tom loved, respected, and admired Kivin and wanted Nicholas to know that. The belief that Nicholas should have a sense of his father led to these conversations. Discussing his father's philosophy, character, profession, successes, goals, values, love of family and friends, sense of responsibility and duty should bring him to life. Nicholas would have a history and a memory of Kivin. The boy may be fatherless, but he would have a wealth of information about his father.

Once Tom took on a task, he delved deeply into it. A characteristic of Tom was list making. He had to write lists for Nicholas's future reading and edification, and he did. The topics included authors, news columnists, books, tips for investing, diets for good nutrition, exercises for fitness. He wanted to cover all bases to prepare Nicholas for adulthood. These plans never materialized. As can happen in the course of events, the best laid plans of mice and men can go astray.

Epilogue
Prophetic Dream

Early in the 1990's, Tom dreamed he came upon an open coffin at a grave site. Staring into the coffin, he found he was looking at himself. Quickly he looked at the grave stone and read the date - June 17, 199? The last number of the year was smudged, illegible. He had dreamed that John F. Kennedy would be shot in Dallas the evening before that assassination. Tom could not totally shake off an ominous feeling about that dream date on the grave stone. He was always wary, expecting some untoward event about that time every year. When we celebrated the millennium, December 31, 1999, his first statement after the usual New Year's wishes was, "We're in 2000, now I don't have to worry about June 17, 199? The nineties are over!"

A short time later Tom bought four pairs of swim trunks in preparation for a summer of swimming, one of his favorite sports dating back to his childhood years spent at Rockaway Beach. This athlete, this marathoner, this one-time triathlete, never used those newly purchased swim trunks. How cruel fate can be! Yes, that year of 199? was accurate. It did not refer to the nineties. Tom succumbed to a massive heart attack on June 12, 2000.

On a not too hot, not too humid morning in the late spring of 2000, Tom's family and friends gathered to bid him a final, fond farewell at a Memorial Service in Our Lady Queen of Peace Church, June 16, 2000. Tom Wing, his brother-in-law, and Ed Tavss, his friend, celebrated Tom's life by recalling his love of family, his many accomplishments, his pranks and shenanigans, his wit, his humor. These were loving and warm remembrances of a man with many parts who had a very short but very full life. The final segment of the memorial was given by me. I alluded to the promises Tom made to me and proudly, happily announced that he kept all of them. Tom was a man who honored his word. Then, to give a sense of the man, to pinpoint the philosophy, the thoughts that compelled him to act, I again referred to the words of Tennyson in "Ulysses." Tom himself underscored these defining lines.

"I am a part of all I met."
"How dull it is to pause, to make an end,
 To rust unburnished, not to shine in use!
As tho' to breathe were life!"
" - - this gray spirit yearning in desire
To follow knowledge like a sinking star,
Beyond the utmost bound of human thought."
"Old age hath yet his honor and his toil,
 Death closes all; but something ere the end,
 Some work of noble note, may yet be done."
      "Come, my friends,
        Tis not too late to seek a newer world."
       "Tho' much is taken, much abides; and tho'
We are not now that strength which in old days
 Moved earth and heaven, that which we are, we are, -
 One equal temper of heroic hearts,
 Made weak by time and fate, but strong on will
 To strive, to seek, to find, and not to yield."

That's my Tom.

Tom lived by these lines from Tennyson. He was driven by a will to strive for his goals, to seek new experiences, to test his limits, and to find an end of noble note. He scored highly in all areas. Tom drank deeply of life.

Yes, Tom, you will always be a part of all you met. Your family, friends, and students are all the better for having known you, for having been touched by you.

But, dear Tom, you forgot one thing. You never promised to grow old with me.